EARLS AND GIRLS

EARLS AND GIRLS

Dramas in High Society

by

Madeleine Bingham

Hamish Hamilton
London

Phototypeset in V.I.P. Sabon by
Western Printing Services Ltd, Bristol
Printed in Great Britain by
Ebenezer Baylis & Son Ltd,
Trinity Press,
London and Worcester

First published in Great Britain 1980
by Hamish Hamilton Limited
Garden House, 57–59 Long Acre, London WC2E 9JZ

British Library Cataloguing in Publication Data
Bingham, Madeleine, *Baroness Clanmorris*
    Earls and girls.
    1. Great Britain – History – Victoria, 1837–1901
    2. Great Britain – History – Edward VII, 1901–1910
    3. Great Britain – Moral conditions
    I. Title
    941.081   DA550

    ISBN 0-241-10270-7

ILLUSTRATIONS

ACKNOWLEDGEMENTS

The author and publishers are grateful to Her Majesty the Queen for permission to reproduce the portrait of H.R.H. The Duke of Cambridge by Winterhalter; to Cassell & Co for permission to quote from the Earl of Rosslyn's *My Gamble with Life* and to Colin G. Winn for permission to reproduce the photograph of the 7th Earl Poulett.

CONTENTS

GENTLEMEN – I GIVE YOU THE LADIES!

Pretty women, elegantly gowned and discreetly lighted, have attracted the attention of gentlemen the other side of the footlights since the days of Nell Gwynn. But most of them were content to be taken into keeping. Marriages were alliances of interest, they represented the solidarity of the ruling class, and interlopers were not welcomed into the charmed circle of the aristocracy.

Several ladies did manage to achieve coronets during the late eighteenth and early nineteenth centuries but they mostly married what Harriette Wilson called 'les beaux restes', rakes on the verge of dissolution. Some ladies, although married, were set up in separate establishments as if they were kept mistresses. One travelled around with a handy parson so that the wedding ring could be slipped on to her finger as soon as the welcome news of the wife's death arrived by travelling coach.

Some actresses supported their retired rakes of husbands, and received very little credit or long term financial assistance for their love and fidelity. Amongst these was the unfortunate Mrs. Dorothy Jordan who, being of genteel blood, although her mother's 'marriage' was disputed, had a yearning towards gentlemen. One of these 'gentlemen' left her with four illegitimate children, and the other, the Duke of Clarence, afterwards the bluff sailor King William IV, honoured her with no less than ten royal bastards.

On the whole, actresses, however respectable they might be in their behaviour, suffered from the taint of backstage raffishness. White bosoms, heavily powdered, could only lead to an assignation amongst the 'patchouli and pink lampshades'.

Today it is difficult to imagine a time when an actress would throw her career to the winds for the sake of marrying a title. The husbands of modern actresses are sometimes contemptuously referred to by their wives' names. The women themselves would not consider ruining a hard-won career for the doubtful use of being referred to as 'your ladyship'. There would be little advantage, either social or monetary, in taking the tickets at the gate of a stately home, or spending one's spare time polishing silver and washing china ready for the summer season. The headlines in modern terms might easily be reversed: 'Film Star marries Peer', and the underlining suggestion made that he was marrying for her money and publicity to prop up his tottering towers.

The attitudes towards stage marriages reflect the times as exactly as any other social phenomenon. In the eighteenth century even the respectable Mrs. Anne Oldfield, for so long the mistress of Arthur Maynwaring Esquire, and mother of his son, found it perfectly natural that he should refuse her the honour of a wedding ring. Yet her contemporaries considered her 'a person whom nature seemed to have solicitously intended for a Court'. She became a leader of modes and manners, and was copied by the very women she represented on the stage. Mr. Maynwaring's friends (of the highest rank) blamed him concerning the affair and 'even Mrs. Oldfield herself frequently represented to him that it was for his Honour and Interest to break off their Alliance'. Anne Oldfield was buried next to Congreve in Westminster Abbey, which would seem to prove that though art may be honoured in death by polite society, in life it could not be socially acknowledged.

There were some half dozen marriages between stage and peerage in the 1840s to the 1870s, but it was not until the 1880s that the whole perspective changed. It was George Edwardes who, long before Ziegfeld, glorified the Girl and altered her social status, and broke the social mould. He was of the opinion that there was magic in the very word 'girl'. It was a magic which succeeded.

Previously, burlesque had been the order of the day. This is not to be confused with American burlesque, which is a strip show. Victorian burlesque was usually a skit on a specific play or opera, or an historical or mythological story. It assumed a remarkable knowledge in the audience of classical drama and opera, European history, and Greek legend, and also great quickness of mind in spotting erudite puns. One burlesque called *Shylock: or the Merchant of Venice Preserv'd*, was described as 'a Jerusalem hearty-joke', and in *The Field of the Cloth of Gold*, Francois Ier rests under a tree and remarks:

> Francis, extended here among the branches
> May well be called — an extension of the franchise.

In Talfourd's *Medea*, the heroine tells Jason she overheard Creusa saying to him, 'If your wife bores you, beat her.' Jason replies:

> You quite mistook her; the reverse meant she:
> Beta in Greek, you know, is letter B. [Let her be.]

2

Magic in the word 'girl'

The largely transvestite casting led later to the principal boy and dame of pantomime. The music was 'borrowed' from the popular songs of the period. When an opera was burlesqued, the music was not necessarily, or even usually, taken from that opera. Gilbert began his theatrical career by writing burlesques, and Planché, H. J. Byron and Talfourd all wrote them. In modern terms the form would entail a piece entitled *Harlequin Jimmy Porter, or the Magic Ironing Board*.

Connie Gilchrist with her hip-length tunic, her skipping-rope and her long slim legs in silken tights was part of burlesque.

Edwardes took over the Gaiety Theatre from Hollingshead, and determined to change the pattern, he invented musical comedy. If Irving made the legitimate stage respectable, Edwardes made the musical stage 'smart' and charming. He banished the fleshings and the tutu, for he realised that a glimpse of ankles and shapely legs from a froth of petticoats was more tantalising and titillating. He created a wonderful veneer. He still employed comediennes and comedians, but the main purpose of the Gaiety was to please. He aimed to please both with the richness of the décor, and the clothes of the women. He toured the provinces searching for the best-looking girls, and then, like some latter-day Hollywood mogul, he

3

groomed them. He employed people to teach them how to talk, how to walk, and, above all, how to dress.

It was said that if a foreigner came to London he would automatically be taken to the Gaiety as the most 'romantic' spot in London. Sometimes with curious results, as when a visiting Eastern potentate offered to buy the entire chorus for his harem. It was hard to persuade him that although the goods were in the shop window, they were strictly not for sale. But as the old stage doorkeeper of the Gaiety recalled, there were other benefits:

> The Maharaja of Cooch Behar thought as little of presenting a lady with a Rolls-Royce, a diamond tiara, or even a furnished villa in the country or up the river as I should of standing a pal a cup of tea.... My stage-door was a miniature Covent Garden on the occasion of a first night. Baskets of the most exquisite flowers from Bond Street filled the hall.... The most beautiful present I ever saw was one sent to Miss Gabrielle Ray. It was a complete grape vine, which had been trained to grow in the shape of a half-hoop, and when it stood in the hall looked like the handle of a gigantic fruit basket. It stood about ten feet high and there were twenty bunches of beautiful black grapes suspended from the vine. It took four men to carry it.

The vine was the work of eight years' tending by a careful gardener. These were some of the fruits of George Edwardes' frou-frou. His emphasis on frou-frou was a deliberate policy, he realised that he was attracting not only the men, thirsty for a glimpse of ankle, but also the women who could see the latest hats with their pleated and ruched chiffons, flowers, fruit, birds, osprey and ostrich feathers, and the 'frocks' with godets, flounces, laces, diamanté and flowers. He insisted that the clothes for his shows should be made by the best designers, and there were to be no more shoddy materials. Silks, laces, and taffetas were of the finest quality. Stockings and parasols must be brought from Paris. Once women began to go about to public restaurants and places of entertainment, the clothes were part of the attraction of the show, and for this reason Edwardes spent without stint. In all of his shows he had what were called the 'Big Eight'. They were the tallest of his flowers – girls who were engaged merely to show off the clothes, as if they were modern photographers' models.

The *Play Pictorials* which later recorded the action of the plays and the songs, also reproduced in the tenderest detail the 'frocks and frills'. Miss Louie Pounds 'altogether charming as a blush Rose' is pictured wearing her lace-trimmed dress bestrewn with roses,

4

while her hero sings: 'Dearest, I need not tell thee all thy dear heart knows, I am the bird that singeth and thou my listening rose.'

The ladies of the period liked to be thought of as listening roses, but the soft-seeming girls with their fur muffs, feathers and furbelows who look so demurely out of the picture postcards of late Victorian and Edwardian London were no longer willing victims, as in past days, of enraptured rakes. As Nan remarks in *A Country Girl* 'I want a man all to myself. There's to be no bites out of my pippin!' The expressions of the whole cast, from the ladies of the chorus to the principals, breathe the atmosphere of a period when girls, however peachlike, were not easy to pluck.

The Little Michus ostensibly taking place in Napoleonic France, was really about two little English damsels, 'Two little hearts beating together, two little heads that are full of fun.' They were also usually full of the idea that it was the plain gold band – or nothing. While the gallant soldiers sang:

> On! on! Gaily riding on
> We are a splendid sight
> To gaze upon
> Setting every heart astir
> With Flash of sword,
> And clink of spur.

They had more in common with the changing of the Guard than the charge of Napoleon's guards. The music may have been Messager, but the background was that of Edwardian London.

Macqueen Pope, looking back on the heady days of the Gaiety girl, was carried away with the idea of the lost beauties of London:

The Gaiety girls were the embodiment of the Romance of London. They were the idol of the youth, rich or poor, of the middle aged and even the elderly. To take a Gaiety girl out to supper, to drive her home in a hansom through the summer night, to propel such a divinity in her laces and silks in a punt at Maidenhead, to take her for a drive in that modern chariot the motor, while her glamour shone through the veils and goggles as a summer sun pierces the morning mist, what more could life offer to a man of that time?

That was the romantic view, the idea which George Edwardes purveyed. There were harsher realities. The 'Big Eight', as they simpered, lifting their delicate skirts, and ogled under their shady hats, were paid more than the girls with talent who danced and sang. Fifteen pounds a week to look beautiful, and wear their clothes with style, as against a mere five pound note for the singing and dancing chorus who added the sparkle and gaiety to the piece. Yet being one of the 'Big Eight' had its disadvantages. Mr. Edwardes' idea was titillation without fulfilment. His girls were welcome to simper over their white fur muffs from the windows of photographers' shops, they could be seen in smart restaurants, but should they put on weight, become pale, pregnant or cease to smile, they were instantly told to pack their frills and make-up, and leave. There was no reprieve for a girl who was too fat, too thin, or involved in scandal. The girls must be as outwardly untouched as the toilettes they wore.

With his impartial respectability, George Edwardes with his actress wife, a wife who had much to be jealous about, and his mistresses, some temporary, and one permanent, reflected the public views to which he catered and pandered. Marie Tempest described Edwardes as wilful, Irish and eccentric but given to the gentlemanly gesture. 'He was Sporting and Dramatic, at this time these two words described a certain class of man. The turf was George Edwardes' wicked mistress and the theatre was his wife. His

George Edwardes – sporting and dramatic

life was a gamble. He was reckless, good company and blessed with fine and convincing self-assurance.'

It was this self-assurance which was the spirit of the age, and spelt success for Edwardes and his Gaiety girls, and his theatre. He was rewarded by the troops of 'mashers' and stage door Johnnies, called the Crutch and Toothpick brigade, who thronged the stage door of the Gaiety and swelled its coffers. The smartness, the chic and the charm were the lure, and the ladies behind the footlights used their froth and frills as bait, and in so doing many of them married into the aristocracy with varying degrees of success.

From the advent of musical comedy, alliances between stage and peerage became more and more frequent. It was deplored amongst the close-knit county and aristocratic families who fought a rear-guard battle against it. But Pinero acclaimed the idea: 'The musical comedy girls will be the salvation of the aristocracy.' Lady Dorothy Nevill voiced the same opinion: 'Many an old family has gained fresh vigour from an infusion of fresh blood, and some of these alliances have been accompanied by considerable romance.' They were also accompanied by a considerable number of court cases.

Lady Dorothy obviously felt that the hearty, healthy girls of the stage who married the stage door Johnnies and the Hon. Algernons brought life and energy into many a stately home, and rejuvenated families which might otherwise have become debilitated and faded from want of sap. It was not perhaps the idea of eugenics, or service to the nation, which prompted these ladies to exchange the shouts of 'Overture and beginners' for the softer sounds of a discreet dinner gong, and the pleasantly spoken, 'Dinner is served, your ladyship.' How nice to feel that it was not a stage butler, intent on upstaging one. Whatever role her ladyship had played in the past, her ladyship was determined to live up to her title.

Many of these ladies became as grand as the women they mimicked on the stage. Marie Tempest was of this company. For it was a time when, as Mr. Maugham wrote, the playgoer demanded a sprinkling of titles in the dramatis personae of a piece. Nature was reflecting art, and the leading ladies who had walked in from painted flats carrying artificial roses from their stage gardens, giving orders to mimic butlers, were able to play these parts 'for real'.

For the soft-seeming girls looking so demurely over the footlights knew which side their beds were buttered, and at a time when it was still possible for a youth to be gilded, they were quite happy to swop the casting couch for the four-poster bed in a stately home.

The lucky ones moved in an atmosphere of great luxury. Drawing-rooms of Louis Seize style with wall treatment vaguely Adam, swagged curtains, scrolled Empire day-beds, gilt furniture, rosewood pianos, wall coverings of silk and bedrooms with canopied beds tricked out in gilt and enclosed with striped satin bed curtains. And everywhere there were hothouse flowers – orchids, carnations, roses – built into pyramids in porcelain pots, or made into looped chains of colour to decorate mantelpieces or enhance dinner tables.

When the ladies went out to dine in public restaurants the settings were equally luxurious. A private supper at the Savoy Hotel included amongst its decorations palm trees growing from the table from which hung baskets of flowers in different bright colours. If the ladies of the theatre seem over decorated, they entirely fitted into their surroundings. If the risks of marrying into the peerage or the purple of gold mining commerce were high, the rewards were rich in every sense of the word.

A private supper at the Savoy Hotel

Some of the girls had their heads turned by the swift change of circumstances. Others managed it with great success, like Gertie Millar, the girl from Bradford, who became Countess of Dudley. Yet others were disillusioned. One wrote that she was cut by the County, and only visited by the vicar (without his wife) once a year.

8

Some never achieved greatness and sued, being paid off by the family with large or small sums, in and out of court. In the days when respectability meant a great deal to a girl some of the frilly ladies who walked from the stage door into the coronetted electric brougham found life in the moated grange could be dull and dispiriting. It needed more than beauty to conquer the County. It needed courage and brains; some of the girls had both these qualities. Others did not.

Some of their stories are histories of stupid young men being victimised, others of girls being subjected to great humiliations. Yet from the old pages of *The Times*, reporting litigation in its pedestrian way, springs the whole world of yesterday. Con-men victimising women, chivalrous men rescuing them. Foolish young men parting with their money. Lovely girls stooping, as always, to folly and 'finding too late that men betray'. Furious fathers threatening their sons. Sad mothers weeping over them, and a whole regiment of useless Algernons and Marmadukes, alleged to be gentlemen, frittering their time away with 'fast women and slow horses'. They lived in their little village bounded by Piccadilly and the Strand, in Clubs called by names like the Corinthian or the Lyric, others put up in 'rooms'. Some were rich and kept their private hansoms, others were mere hangers-on profiting by the folly of others. And always there were the girls. Girls who could be charming, or predatory, vulnerable or grasping, generous or cold-hearted. Girls who used their beauty as a gift, or a trap.

The whole world of the earls and girls has gone, and yet their stories reveal much of the human heart, from the Duke who married his Columbine and remained faithful unto death, to the lady whose heart was mended to the tune of £50,000 golden sovereigns.

BUTTERFLY ON THE WHEEL
or
The Case of Countess Belle

The facts of the case of Countess Belle, or Lady Dunlo, as she was at the time of the court proceedings against her, seem simple. A furious father, the Earl of Clancarty, was trying to annul or set aside her marriage to his son.

Yet if one reads the original *Times'* court reports a completely different, more vivid, and stranger picture springs from the old columns. It is that of a chivalrous man, a pusillanimous youth, an unscrupulous father, and a lovely, but vulnerable lady. It also throws up an odd amalgam of useless clubmen, not the amiable fools whose prototype is Bertie Wooster, but a less fragrant and less funny variety. The stage door Johnnies of books of old theatrical reminiscences turned up with immense baskets of orchids with five pound notes concealed in their petals. The beautiful girls then kept the flowers, and sent back the money via an ex-Army stage door-keeper who was there to protect the girls from harm. It all seemed idyllic. The girls were pure, and the men chivalrous. The case of Countess Belle shows a different picture.

Belle Bilton was born about 1867, the daughter of a recruiting sergeant in the Royal Engineers. When the sergeant retired he became attached in some humble capacity to the Garrison Theatre in Woolwich. His wife acted as an amateur on the same stage. On account of their parents' connection with the Garrison Theatre the two girls, Isabel and her sister, Florence (Belle and Flo), were attracted to theatre life, and showing some ability they went on the stage, both from inclination, and presumably to help out the family budget at a time when ex-sergeants' pensions were as humble as their situation in life. Belle was about thirteen. She was more beautiful than her sister Flo; from her photographs she had a fragile quality, but no doubt her tougher sister was better able to cope with the ups and downs of their touring life in the provinces, and protected Belle.

The recruiting sergeant's two daughters had been in their turn recruited by Mr. Charles Barnard and his wife, to sing in the chorus of an all-child production of *Les Cloches de Corneville* at Elliot Galer's Theatre in Reading. There were seventy-eight children in the cast and twelve adults to keep them in order. Mrs. Barnard, like Mrs. Bateman, Irving's employer at the Lyceum in London, supervised the wardrobe and made many of the clothes. Both ladies seem to have approved of economies. But Mrs. Barnard was not unmindful of the welfare of the children entrusted to her. She organised a travelling school which the children had to attend. They were taught the three R's – reading, writing and arithmetic – music, dancing, and, it was alleged, French. But as Flo and Belle referred to the piece in which they were playing as 'the Clocks', the teaching of French by Mrs. Barnard would appear to be doubtful.

From Reading the children toured in 'the Clocks' – to the Gaiety for matinées under John Hollingshead, then for a long peregrination from one grim Victorian provincial town to another, ending at Galer's Opera House in Leicester. December 1881 found them at the Theatre Royal, Glasgow in *Dick Whittington*. From then on for the next four or five years they toured the provinces gradually building up their reputation, always appearing together as the Sisters Bilton. During one of their tours a manager who was looking for new talent saw them. 'Sisters' acts were very popular at the time, and at last they had arrived – they were booked to star at the Alhambra and Empire Theatres in the West End of London. An 'artiste' who appeared on the same bill as the Sisters Bilton about this time remembered what a great sensation they had made when they first sang and danced at the Empire. But the greater attraction of the two was always Belle. Overnight she became a celebrity. She was interviewed by reporters. Her opinions on marriage and morals, on frocks and frills were canvassed. She was not only interviewed, she was photographed and fêted. The postcards of this delicate girl appeared in all the photographers' shops, and it was said that they sold even better than those of the Jersey lily, Mrs. Langtry.

Seymour Hicks, who knew Belle at this time, wrote of the fun which was 'fast and furious at the old Pelican Club', and of how the stars of the music hall would come round to join in after the show. 'I was introduced to Belle Bilton – she was sweetly pretty, her beauty being of the wistful delicate type, her sister was on the more robust side.' The Sisters Bilton were, wrote Mr. Hicks, 'one of the most popular of the Sisters acts' and the 'little ditties they warbled were inane, and always followed with a stereotyped class of simultane-

11

ous movement chivalrously called dancing by their hosts of admirers'. The chorus of their most famous song ran:

> We're fresh, fresh as the morning,
> Sweeter than new mown hay,
> We're fresh, fresh, fresh as the morning
> And just what you want today.

Judging from the strength of the love she inspired in her suitors this was only too true of the lovely Belle.

Belle Bilton. Her beauty was of the wistful, delicate type

In 1886 at one of these parties after the show, when all was champagne, soft lights and sparkling eyes, and the mashers about town mingled with the beautiful Bilton sisters relaxing after their double act, Belle met Alden Weston. He told her he was an officer in the Army. The 1880s was a time when Army officers had a certain social cachet, and after all, Belle, the daughter of a humble recruiting sergeant, had seen these grand epauletted gods shouting commands at their men on the parade ground at Chatham, or prancing

12

on their horses when off-duty. She was impressed with the idea of marrying an officer and gentleman. It was a step up. It was said that she was warned against Alden Weston. No doubt the practical Flo spotted him as what was called in those days 'a wrong 'un' from the first. But Belle was only nineteen and in love for the first time; knowing nothing about Alden she set up house with him first in a grand flat in Victoria Street and then later in Dover Street, Piccadilly. He seemed, as she later put it, 'very flush of money'. No expense was spared, although he does not seem to have suggested either that she should marry him, or give up her music hall engagements. The idyll with Weston lasted little more than a year. Then disasters fell thick and fast. Belle discovered that she was pregnant. She also discovered that Weston was married. And shortly afterwards he was convicted of fraud. The money he was so grandly splashing about was not his, and he was sent to Holloway. It turned out that he was already known to Scotland Yard as a confidence trickster, and had been in the dock several times. The gentlemanly exterior was as fraudulent as everything else about him. But it was very easy for a girl with no social background, who did not have a steely sensible character, to fall into the arms of the first attractive 'cad' who laid siege to her. And gentlemen were apt to lay siege to Belle, as it was to be proved afterwards. Her sad beauty and soft vulnerable quality seem to have had a disastrous effect both on the hearts of men, and on the course of her own life.

In February of 1888, when she was already three months pregnant, still at the Empire Theatre dancing and singing of being 'fresh, fresh as the morning dew', she was asked to supper with a Major Noah, and introduced to Isidor Wertheimer. Wertheimer was a very well-heeled dealer in what was contemptuously called by some bric-à-brac, and by those who sold them *objets de vertu*. The Wertheimers were in business in Bond Street, where they also lived. Isidor had been left a great deal of money by his grandfather, which led to certain difficulties with his father and uncle who did not seem to appreciate the terms of the grandfather's will, as relatives so often do not.

But Belle had met her saviour. Isidor, like so many others, fell immediately and headlong in love with her. She did not deceive him as to her condition, for when he proposed marriage to her she told him of her predicament. He was not only heartsick and sympathetic, but practical and helpful. By April of 1888, she was already over four months pregnant and could hardly sing about being as fresh as the morning dew any longer, nor was it advisable that she should prance about the stage in a sisters' act. Isidor took charge. He told her how desperately he felt for her situation, he would do anything for her, he said. Unlike most people who promise, the chivalrous Isidor kept his promises. He took a house for her at Maidenhead. He made all the arrangements for her lying-in, he arranged for her sister and brother-in-law to live with her at Farleigh Lodge, Maidenhead so that her reputation should be preserved, and she should not be seen to be living under his protection as his kept mistress. And very sweetly, he went with her to the baby linen shop to choose the layette for the coming child.

The baby was a boy, born in July of 1888. After the birth the delicate Belle was very ill, and had to have more than one operation. When she had recovered a little, Isidor decided to take her abroad for a holiday. His friend, a Mr. Grylls, booked rooms for them in Trouville and Paris, and indeed he stayed at the same hotels. He later admitted that he had also offered to marry Belle.

Isidor, still desperately in love, also continued to propose, but Belle refused. She was not in love with Isidor – or for that matter with Mr. Grylls. She appreciated, deeply appreciated, all his kindness, but she was not in love. It would seem that Belle, like many ladies before and since, equated true love with the violent physical attraction she had felt for Alden Weston. She was still, in spite of all that had happened, writing affectionate letters to Weston, and on one occasion Wertheimer had driven her to Holloway to see him in prison.

Isidor seems to have been not only a persistent, but a very long-suffering suitor. But gradually Belle came to her senses about Alden Weston, and eventually her passion faded. She went back to living in digs under the name of 'Mrs. Weston', but the baby sickened, and Wertheimer suggested that the best plan would be to rent a house 'out of town'. He leased 63 Avenue Road, St. John's Wood. Beyond Regent's Park not far from Primrose Hill the air was fresher, and the child and his nurse could be accommodated.

The house no longer exists, but from the remaining grand villas, it is possible to imagine it, a three-storied stucco house with mansard windows in the roof, double fronted with a flight of steps leading up to a front door protected by a porch, a carriage entrance with two gates, and at the back a stable yard. Here Isidor set Belle up in fine style with her sister and brother-in-law as chaperones; here he kept his private hansom, his dog cart, and his carriage, with five horses for driving and riding. There were servants to wait on Belle, a black page boy, a stable boy, a coachman, a housekeeper, and parlour-maid, as well as housemaids. Isidor had not only rescued Belle, but had provided her with a softly comfortable feather bed. Unfortunately for Wertheimer, this he did not share. He accompanied Belle to the theatre, clop-clopping round Regent's Park towards Oxford

Street and finally Leicester Square. After the show they would have supper at the Café Royal (in one of the public rooms – naturally), and then she was driven home in his private hansom, his crest on the shiny doors and his initial on the well-polished harness. Miss Bilton was being comforted in style.

At this time, no doubt, Isidor must have felt that his devotion, his patience, and his refusal to push Belle into a more intimate relationship than she deeply felt, would in the end be rewarded. He did spend nights at 63 Avenue Road, but always chaperoned by Belle's relations, and he always occupied his own separate room. But his orthodox Jewish family were incensed by the whole episode. His father thought him a fool for falling in love with a pretty face, more especially as he seemed to be getting less than his reward in return for the lavish expense of the establishment in St. John's Wood. One can imagine the lengthy conferences of the Wertheimer family intent on getting their son to see sense.

In the spring of 1889, they decided to send Isidor to New York on business for the family firm. It was then that Belle met Viscount Dunlo, heir to the Earl of Clancarty. She seems to have been as violently attracted to him as he was to her. It is hard nowadays to understand what a title meant to people lower down the social scale. It had a glow, an attraction – behind the ordinary-looking young lord trembled escutcheons, knights in armour, and all the panoply described by Sir Walter Scott. Belle was a simple girl, and she believed all Lord Dunlo told her.

Vesta Tilley said that she remembered the courtship of Viscount Dunlo – how he used to call for the beautiful Belle after the show, and outside in the street he kept his private hansom cab – waiting to drive her off to supper. Miss Tilley was, of course, wrong. It was not the noble lord's private hansom cab, it was Isidor Wertheimer's – Isidor who had been banished to the other side of the Atlantic by his family. While Isidor was absent, William Le Poer Trench, Viscount Dunlo (known to his friends as Fred) was whispering sweet nothings into the ear of Belle, feeding her after the show (on credit), and then driving her home to the grand house in the fresh air of St. John's Wood, paid for, and staffed by the faithful Isidor. He seems to have made extensive use of Isidor's carriages, as well as proposing marriage to Isidor's loved one.

But Isidor himself had not been entirely idle. He was sending cables (in code) proposing marriage to Belle: 'Come to Paris with Seymour [her brother-in-law] and marry me there.' But Belle, dazzled by the grandeur of her new suitor and already half in love, cabled back: 'Don't want to be married.'

While Belle was being thus assiduously wooed by Fred Dunlo,

Seymour and Flo were less than pleased about this youth's coming to destroy Belle for love, and for the second time. They had had enough trouble with the cad Alden Weston, and now she had in Isidor, a steady kind follower of twenty-six, a much more sensible age, who could do everything for her, and this callow youth of twenty was proposing to upset the apple cart. Seymour went bull-headed at the whole problem. He told Flo that if Fred 'came after Belle' he would punch his head in. Seymour was obviously not a man who was over impressed with coronets. He also went round to confront Fred in his rooms. Fred was absent, but Seymour, baulked from punching his head in, met Marmaduke Wood, a croney of Fred's. 'Marmy' told Seymour a few home truths — marriage between Fred and Belle was highly unlikely, Clancarty would never give his consent. Marmey added a few uncomplimentary remarks about the whole idea of marriage into Seymour's family — 'speaking very roughly on the subject'. Seymour was quite capable of rough speaking himself, and repeated that it would be a good thing if Fred ceased 'coming after Belle'. Marmey Wood and Seymour had the measure of one another. Later Fred was still protesting to Seymour that his father would give him an allowance, but these protestations cut no ice with Seymour. He believed neither in talk of allowances, nor that Belle's honour could be protected, for he was quite certain that Clancarty was determined to destroy Belle's hopes. In some senses he was right.

He was also quite right about Clancarty who had hardly been idle. He had heard much earlier that Fred had got in with a 'bad lot' in London. Previously he had tried to make a man of Fred by getting him into the Army, but Fred does not seem to have been very bright, and could not pass even the simple Army entrance exams. The only way round this impasse, was to get Fred a commission in the Militia. So in April 1889, about the time Fred met Belle, the Earl had arranged for his son to go into the Militia as a way of getting some training, and perhaps later being able to get into a good Regiment by a side door.

Fred decided not to turn up for his training. He had already met Belle, and army training was not at all the thought uppermost in his mind.

The Earl, his whiskers alerted to trouble, had a discussion with his Countess, and they made plans for their errant son. They would send him round the world for a couple of years, until he should be weaned from his bad companions, settle down, and marry some nice suitable 'gel'. A man called Robinson was engaged to accompany Lord Dunlo on this world trip, and the voyage was to commence in July of 1889.

Whether it was the threat of the world voyage, or the frantic physical attraction they felt for one another which pushed the twenty-two-year-old Belle, and the twenty-year-old Fred into the final step, it is difficult to say. In desperation they went off on 10 July to Hampstead Registry Office – and were married. The Earl was not told, 'battling' Seymour was not told, poor Isidor was not told. Only Flo knew that Belle had finally capitulated and become Lady Dunlo.

Ironically, it may have been Isidor's desperate cables which finally pushed the couple over the brink, for later in court, Fred admitted that he had written to Belle saying that Wertheimer was broken-hearted but that he, Fred had won the prize – and that was the fortune of war. Not that Fred intended to fight any wars, not even with his father.

After the marriage the couple separated. Fred went back to the Coburg Hotel, and Belle to 63 Avenue Road. He appears to have told Belle that he had been arguing for two hours with his father to get his consent to the marriage. He also convinced Belle that as soon as he became twenty-one, which was in six months' time, Clancarty would give them enough money to live on, and set them up in a house of their own. Later none of this was proved to be true, but Belle, a loving and gullible girl, believed it. She now had her 'lines', and all would be well in the end. Fred also said he had told his father categorically that whatever happened he would *never* marry anyone else, and now he had proved it by signing the marriage certificate.

What Fred had not told her was that his parents knew nothing about the marriage at all. But all of them reckoned without the *Pall Mall Gazette* which published a report of the marriage on 15 July. On the same day Fred and Belle went to the Victoria Hotel where they stayed for the first time together as man and wife.

The following day Fred wrote a letter to his father.

My dear Papa,

When I returned back from Ranelagh this morning, Mama showed me the *Pall Mall Gazette* about my marriage. I laughed at it, and came straight away, because there was no use in saying anything to her. But I must tell you the truth. I believe I really am married and there is no use in denying it. Why I did it I don't know. I have no excuse to make. I can't say I was drunk. I don't think I was, but I believe I must be rather off my head during the last few months. I must say one thing, several of my friends, Mr. Benzon, Lord Alfred Osborne, Mr. Wood [Marmey Wood] Mr. Grand and especially Mr. Scott have been most kind to me. They all went, unknown to me to various lawyers and solicitors and did their level best to find out if there was any flaw in the marriage, thinking it might not be valid as I am under age. I know, of course, I have played the devil, and am truly sorry for it (I mean for you, Mama, Kathleen &c), as for myself I don't care a rap. No one is to blame except myself. What is to be done I don't know. The sooner I go away the better. I should like to remain abroad as long as possible. What is to become of her – I must leave to you, and I will respect your wishes in every way. One thing I can tell you – she is very quiet.

Fred, subservient to his father, speaks of the girl he had so precipitately married as if she were a tamed horse.

She will do whatever you wish in every way. I now see clearly what an awful thing I have done, but as I said before, I don't care a rap for myself, but only for you, Mama & c. I have now made a clean breast of it, and feel much happier. I would have told you some days ago only I could never summon up pluck enough to do so, and do not expect any forgiveness from you because I only too clearly know what I have done. It is done now, and I am much afraid that nothing will get me out of it. Will you write an answer to me here. [He was writing from the Burlington Hotel, and not from the Victoria Hotel where he was staying with his wife.]
    Tell me what you want me to do and I will faithfully do it. One thing I would like to say and it is true, no blame can be attached to the girl, it is all my fault. Please understand that what I want to know is what your wishes are now. One thing I am certain of is that the *Pall Mall* had no right to publish it like that without permission. Write please immediately here and tell me your wishes, and believe me always your affectionate son,
                                    Dunlo.

Clancarty was certain that he could upset the marriage, if not by having it annulled, then in some other way. He had decided to carry on with his plan to send Fred off round the world. The berths were engaged for Dunlo and his travelling companion Mr. Robinson. They were to sail from Tilbury on 19 July, exactly nine days after the wedding.
    Apart from tearing his son away from the arms of his new wife, Clancarty had been busy combing the papers for gossip about her. There were a number of journals at the time which specialised in scandal and spicy bits about the goings-on of clubmen, peers about town, and ladies who pirouetted on the stage; these appeared in

papers like *The Hawk* and *Man of the World*. Clancarty discovered a report that Belle had had not one, but three children, and added that if Fred went away she would most certainly produce another. In fact, Belle had already told her young husband about her child, but this does not seem to have made any difference to his love for her which was absolutely genuine. But girls are one thing, and fathers who hold the purse strings are another. Fred was in a fix. He was telling Belle that he was arranging for her to come round the world with him, that he had been down to Tilbury and engaged their berths, and that his father was coming round to the idea of the marriage. Clancarty had been told that Belle wanted to go with her husband, but he would 'have nothing to do with such an arrangement'.

The day of the round-the-world voyage approached. On the night of 18 July, Fred met Belle at the stage door of the Empire and escorted her back to their hotel. He seemed very depressed. This was not surprising for he had been reassuring his wife right up to the eve of his voyage that she would be coming with him. She had implored him not to go alone, and he had promised faithfully that he would never, never leave her. He dropped her at the Victoria Hotel and said he wanted to be alone to think – he went off into the night and did not get back till five o'clock in the morning. Had he gone off to drink, and be comforted by his friends Lord Alfred and Marmey Wood at his old haunts the Corinthian, Evans, or the Lyric Club? When he did come back in the grey hours of dawn, he finally plucked up his courage and told Belle he was going that morning – and without her.

Belle broke down. 'Who is to look after me?' she asked him, and added that she and her sister had only one engagement, for ten guineas a week between them. What was to become of her? Fred, under sailing orders from his father, had no reply except to say to the sobbing girl, that his father would give him no money unless he went away, but, if he did, when he was twenty-one an allowance would be forthcoming. This was untrue.

But Clancarty had other plans. He did not believe in the validity of the marriage, and was quite convinced that once his son was out of the way, Belle would be certain, as the current phrase had it, 'to go wrong'. He went off to consult the law, and was put on to Sir George Lewis who took his instructions, and promptly made arrangements to have Belle watched. Once married, she had left Wertheimer's house in Avenue Road, and gone into lodgings taking her child and the nurse with her. She was living in Conduit Street off Hanover Square, and still singing and dancing at the Empire, though hardly, it must be thought, feeling as fresh as new mown

Fred in later life

hay. She was also being shadowed by the two private detectives hired by Lewis, the Clarke brothers, who lurked in the street near her digs and followed her to the theatre.

Belle's stay in Conduit Street did not last long, for the landlady took exception to her large dog, and she had to move to Bennet Street, St. James's. Here further troubles awaited her. Alden Weston, now out of gaol, was spoiling for a fight with someone, and had picked on Wertheimer as an excuse. Weston turned up at her lodgings with a solicitor called Abrahams and there was a row. He forced his way up to Belle's rooms and confronted her. She ordered him out of the house. The upshot of the fracas was that she had a bruised forehead. She said later in court that she had knocked it on a door, but ladies who get punched in the face are generally said to have walked into doors. Abrahams, perhaps softened by seeing Belle, apologised for the intrusion, and he and Alden left the house.

What Alden wanted to get out of Belle from this interview is unclear. Perhaps he had not heard of her marriage, and hoped to blackmail the well-heeled Wertheimer for some ready cash. But the landlady, a Mrs. de Palma, was becoming tired of histrionics. It was no advertisement for her highly respectable rooms in St. James's if ex-gaol birds turned up to make scenes, and beat up her lodgers, and outside in the street the two Clarkes were ever-watchful taking down Belle's movements in their grubby notebooks. The landlady gave Belle notice. Belle dissolved into tears, and asked Mrs. de Palma: 'Where am I to go?' Like Fred Dunlo, Mrs. de Palma had no answer to Belle's problems. She admitted that Lady Dunlo's conduct had always been perfectly ladylike, but all the same she must go. That was final.

By this time Wertheimer had arrived back from America. He had been visiting Belle at her lodgings and accompanying her backwards and forwards to the Empire where she was playing. When he heard that she was being pestered by Weston, he came round and took her away – back to Avenue Road in his hansom cab. He may not have been a knight in shining armour, but he was a compassionate man with a great love for Belle. She was back in her comfortable nest with someone to look after her, and always a sister or a cousin to chaperone her. But outside in the road there were still the two Clarkes busily watching and hoping for the worst. But Wertheimer was circumspect; although he drove her backwards and forwards to the theatre he never stayed at the house.

The picture which afterwards emerged in court about Belle and Isidor at this time is how they lunched, dined and drove out together in his dog cart, or in the evenings in his private hansom. They drove 'tandem' to Hampton Court, to Surrey, or down to Barnes or

Richmond. Accompanying a pretty woman on a bright day in a dog cart trotting along drawn by a good piece of horse flesh, Isidor could not be blamed for thinking that devotion and fidelity might win the girl in the end. At moments the case, as later reported, recalls the picture of the disgraced Irene being pursued by Soames in *The Forsyte Saga*. But Belle was more of a victim than Irene. Belle always wanted someone to care for her, perhaps she believed the sad sentimental ballads of the period which sang of men being kind and loving and girls pure.

Belle wrote of all her outings to the absent Fred. She had walked down Bond Street with Isidor who had bought her a big bunch of roses. She had seen two cigarette cases in a shop with a picture on them of herself dancing. She had bought two of them, one she was sending to him, the other she had given to Isidor. She reassured her darling Fred how heart-broken she was that they were not together – and she loved him, and him alone.

The months went by – August, September, October, Belle continued to dance and to assure Fred by every mail of her undying love, and Fred wrote back in equally fervent tones. But all the time the Clarkes were busy noting when Belle drove out with Isidor, where she lunched, where she dined. She went off to dance in Manchester with her sister, and Isidor visited her there several times. She was down at Brighton playing the name part in a comic opera called *Venus* and had ridden over to Plumpton races with Isidor, who had given her a horse for which he had paid 200 guineas. She wrote naively to her husband of all her activities, making no secret of the kindnesses with which Isidor showered her. But all the time the travelling Fred knew perfectly well that she was being followed, and that his father was quite determined to rid the Clancarty family of her. But even Fred seems, at this point, to have decided that it might be as well to give her a tiny hint of her predicament.

He wrote: 'Don't go too much about with W. People will talk; not that I care, for I trust you with all my heart and soul.' He might have trusted her but he had left her with neither money nor a place to live. He was aware that the only way she could make a living was by dancing at three music halls every night. The unfortunate Belle, aware of the shadowing, was unaware that it was tacitly condoned by her loving and trusting Fred. He wrote from Adelaide that he had been bothered by reporters who had come to interview him, because it had been stated in various newspapers that his father was trying to have the marriage annulled. 'What bosh! Why the deuce the public can't leave us alone – I can't see. It is nothing to them.'

But meanwhile the Clarkes went about their business, noting and scribbling. They later said in court that they were employed by their father, who in his turn was employed by their grandfather, who had been given the job by Sir George Lewis. No one was admitting to being hired by Lord Clancarty. As far as the Clarkes knew it was Lord Dunlo who had engaged them to shadow his wife. By the end of the year, in November of 1889, Lord Clancarty had convinced himself that the worst had – very fortunately – happened. Adultery was certainly being committed – he had the proofs in the notebooks of the Clarke brothers. On 17 December the wretched Fred, who had been getting letters from his father by every mail retailing every unfortunate fact of Belle's past, received the petition for divorce on account of Belle's adultery with Isidor Emanuel Wertheimer. Fred, Lord Dunlo, Belle's loving husband signed it, he also signed an affidavit stating that he believed the facts stated to be true, and dutifully sent both documents back to his father in London.

How Clancarty's face must have been suffused with triumph once he had the precious documents in his hand.

But Fred, ever wavering Fred, sat down the following day, and wrote to Belle from the Warrigal Club, Sydney.

My own darling wife,
    I last wrote to you from Melbourne, and told you I was about to commence my journey homewards. I left Melbourne on Saturday on the S.S. *Arawa* and arrived here on Monday. We leave here on Friday for Brisbane and sail from that place in the *Jumna* on the 24th. Many thanks for your letter of November 9th. So you think do you that I get plenty of fun out of my exile? You think I forget you, Belle. I do nothing but think of you all day, and dream of you all night. I love you, I love you truly. I never look at anyone else. I never think of anyone else but you, my pretty Belle. If you did not care for me, I should – I do not know what I should do. Do you remember in a letter you wrote me dated, I think, November 1st, you said that George Lewis had hinted that he was going to write out to me about you? Well, he did. I got the letter the other day in Melbourne, and I will give you the exact words of the letter. 'Acting under instructions from your father, I have caused Lady Dunlo to be watched. From the reports of the detectives submitted to me I have no doubt of the guilt of your wife, who daily and hourly is in the company of Mr. Isidor Wertheimer.' He then went on to say that if an action for divorce were taken a decree was certain to be given in my favour. Now, Belle, I don't believe a word of it.

Fred was hardly the hero 'white all through' portrayed in the plays of the period. He then went on to justify himself in his own eyes.

> Don't be angry with me. I must say that I think you must have been about too much with Mr. Wertheimer. You know that every person talks whenever they get a chance and, of course, seeing you with Wertheimer they have begun to jabber. Belle, I love you dearly and for goodness sake don't give every idiot a chance to waggle his tongue. George Lewis is not, I think, a man who would go and write to me like that for nothing. You see his letter is a pretty strong one. But my darling, I love you with my whole soul, and don't believe a word of it, but don't give these idiots the chance to talk so much.

Fred concluded with the jolly news that he had been out yachting on a forty ton schooner, and they had had a very good sail. It was jolly good boating weather for Fred, but hardly for Belle. He ended by assuring Belle of his undying love, he hoped that she would get his letter by the end of January and he would be home very soon after that. 'Now au revoir and remember Belle that I always, always and for *ever* love you, my darling. So believe me ever your own loving husband

FRED.'

The same day as she sighed over this letter Belle was served with a divorce petition. She wrote frantically to Lord Clancarty asking him to see her so that she could clear herself of the charges, but he did not reply.

Meanwhile poor Isidor was in further hot water. Alden Weston had reappeared and was forging cheques against his bank account, and getting them cashed by a money-lender. He was also forging letters from Belle and from Wertheimer which were later read out in court. Weston seems to have been very handy at forgeries because even the bank clerks who were called as witnesses appear to have been deceived.

The forgery case was a presage of the battle which was later to ensue between Belle and Lord Clancarty. The question of her relations with Isidor came up in the forgery case, for amongst his masterpieces Weston had written a letter purporting to be from Isidor.

> My dearest Belle, I send by Herbert the cheque you asked for, of

24

£300 which I have post-dated 15th. Please don't use it unless by your own people. Am at Café Royal waiting for you. Have taken box for boxing competition.

In haste, always your Isidore.

But Alden Weston had made several mistakes. He had put an 'e' on the name Isidor, endorsed the cheque 'Isabelle Dunlo' instead of I. M. P. Dunlo, and when Belle gave evidence about the letter, she said she had never been at a boxing match in her life, adding that she 'would have been afraid to go to one' – which was typical of her nervous and vulnerable character. Unlike Flo she was not 'robust'. It was also proved that a servant dismissed by Isidor had stolen papers from Avenue Road, which enabled Weston to fake the signatures and writing of both Belle and Isidor.

No doubt the Earl was delighted that Belle should in this way be publicly exposed as being mixed up with a forger who had admitted having 'close relations' with her. Forged cheques written in public houses on the way to Richmond, pawnbrokers who alleged they had been cheated – it was all good grist to the mill of blackening Belle's character before the divorce case actually started. This additional case had fallen very opportunely on 5 July; the petition for the Dunlo divorce was set down to be heard before Sir James Hannen, the President of the Divorce Court at the end of the same month.

It began on 24 July 1890 and lasted for six days. Mr. Lockwood Q.C. and Mr. Searle defended Belle, Mr. Gill appeared for Isidor. But the Earl had found no less than two Q.Cs. to appear for his pawn – Fred – Sir C. Russell and Mr. Inderwick.

Such a panoply of legal talent, and such spicy bits about high life and low life, titled ladies, music hall performers, forgers, and beautiful women set up in rich houses in St. John's Wood with horses and carriages, had caused intense excitement among the public. So much so that the President threatened to have everyone banned from the court. The corridors must be kept clear, the crowds of sightseers were impeding not only learned counsel, but also the witnesses in the case. And the witnesses provided a spectacle in themselves. There were the two Clarkes (with notebooks), a black pageboy employed by Wertheimer, assorted servants, stableboys at inns in Barnes, waiters in London and Paris. It was very titillating for all except the weak-willed Fred, and the sad Belle at the centre of the furore.

Sir C. Russell began by sounding the right note of *snobisme*. The respondent was a young woman who sang and danced displaying her considerable talents and attractions in the music halls of the metropolis, the petitioner was, of course, the eldest son of the Earl of Clancarty and came of age on 27 December 1889.

Most of the first days of the case were taken up by mulling over the tale of Belle's relations with Weston and the birth of her child. Learned counsel for the defence tied the Clarkes up in a few knots, for although they alleged that they had seen Isidor and Belle hugging and kissing they could not produce notes to prove it. Henry John Clarke said he had seen Mr. Wertheimer driving backwards and forwards from the Café Royal, but he had to admit that he had never seen them except in the *public* rooms. He also alleged that he had seen Wertheimer in his shirt sleeves in the bedroom at 63 Avenue Road, and had a picture in his mind of Lady Dunlo calling across the stable yard to the coachman from the same window. But the picture in Clarke's mind was not enough for the Judge, and he despatched the Clarkes to find their original notes to see if they could prove all the intimacies they had been describing so vividly.

Charles Nunn, a cab driver, formerly in service with Mr. Wertheimer as his coachman, was called. Yes, he was accustomed to drive Mr. Wertheimer and Lady Dunlo all over the place, to the Empire

OUR CABBIES

'I would have done the same thing – if I had had the chance.'

26

Theatre and cafés. Before the marriage he had seen Mr. Wertheimer put his arm round Lady Dunlo, once or twice, but he did not think anything of that – and he added perkily 'I would have done the same thing – if I had had the chance.' No, he had never seen them kissing. At Avenue Road they had had a dog cart, a private hansom, another carriage, and five horses. Lord Dunlo was accustomed to use the private hansom after he began his visits to the house. Yes, Mr. Wertheimer's crest was on the doors of the hansom and his initials on the harness. This was an unfortunate piece of evidence for Fred, for he had already said he was not aware that the carriage was Isidor's.

But the second day gave the spectators their money's worth when clubman Mr. Marmaduke Wood was called. He announced himself as an officer in the Militia, and described his status as a gentleman of private means. It was not, as it was later to transpire, what learned counsel on the other side proved him to be.

Cross-examined by Mr. Gill (for Isidor) he admitted he had seen a good deal of Lord Dunlo since his return from Australia. They were, as a matter of fact, living at the Corinthian Club. And Benzon? Well, he was a member. Mr. Gill replied sharply: 'Of course! He was one of your lot!'

Learned Counsel, Mr. Lockwood (for Lady Dunlo) said he himself happened to be a member of the Lyric Club, and there had been some talk of the case amongst the members. Learned Counsel continued:

'Did you in the presence of persons make a statement as to your own improper intimacy with this lady?'

'Not that I recollect.'

'I again ask you, Sir, as an officer in her Majesty's militia, whether you did not say in public that you had had such an intimacy with her?'

'I don't remember.'

'Did you say that Lord Alfred Osborne had such an intimacy with her?'

'I might have said that.'

'Did you say that you and Lord Alfred Osborne and Lord Dunlo tossed up for her to decide which of you should have her, and the lot fell on Lord Dunlo?'

'I stated that, and it was so.'

'Is it true, sir, that you ever had anything to do with this woman in your life?'

'No, I never had.'

'Did you suggest that Lord Alfred Osborne had?'

'Yes.'

27

'He is not in the country I believe?'

'No, he is in Ceylon.'

'Ah – I thought he was not in England. Were you sober when you were talking of this matter at the Lyric Club last night?'

'Yes. I was sober.'

'Then surely you cannot forget whether you stated that you yourself had been improperly intimate with this lady, when you now admit it is not true that you ever have been?'

'I will not swear that I did not say it.'

Here the President intervened. 'Can you swear whether you did, or did not say it?'

Marmey Wood was cornered and added weakly: 'I will swear that I did not say it – so far as I am aware.'

Learned Counsel, Mr. Lockwood then proceeded to slice Marmy Wood into a very fine tilth indeed, and ended with a flourish.

'Then you suggest that – in a public Club – you may have told a lie?'

Marmey: 'That I may have told a lie? I hope not.'

Mr. Lockwood: 'I have done with you, sir.'

Marmey Wood may have been in with the right set, but he was in the wrong club on the wrong night, for Learned Counsel had overheard his boasts.

Having heard all the evidence (including Isidor's which came at the end of the case) the President summed up. He outlined the story of Belle, of her betrayal by Weston and his imprisonment. There was no doubt in his mind that the respondent (Lady Dunlo) at that moment was in an unhappy and pitiable state, enough to excite the compassion of anyone. It had been suggested in court that Wertheimer had been actuated by motives other than philanthropy in taking the house at Maidenhead. This was an uncharitable view.

The President's wise words as they fell on the ears of the avidly waiting public reflected the current feeling for the needs of a woman. Lord Clancarty had not acted correctly. It was a very serious thing that any married woman should be deprived of 'the protection and society of her husband ... he did not take any pains to keep Lady Dunlo from temptation, but had avowed in the witness box that when his son was leaving he not only did not care whether she fell, but would be pleased if she did.'

He had equally harsh words for the weak-willed Fred – what was he doing writing love letters to his wife avowing that he trusted her, and by the same mail sending off affidavits to the effect that his wife was guilty of adultery? Nothing that Lord Dunlo said or did was important in the case. He was a mere cipher and puppet in the hands of his father. The case depended on whether Wertheimer and Lady Dunlo had committed adultery. The President ended by remarking that he was thankful the task had fallen on the jury and not on himself.

The jury retired and after only fifteen minutes, returned the verdict that Belle and Isidor had not committed adultery, and costs were awarded to Isidor.

The long ordeal was over. Like the demon king the Earl retired hurt. Even *The Times* was severe with him. He had failed to rid the house of Clancarty of a distasteful alliance and behaved to 'this woman hardly, unfeelingly, and almost cynically.... It is Lord Clancarty's own fault if his conduct is set down in some quarters as a piece of sharp practice.' He had sent his son round the world apparently careless of 'the terrible temptations which assail a handsome woman deprived of her husband's protection, and marked out by her calling for the attentions of every wealthy libertine.' In 1890 ladies were expected to need a shoulder to cry on, and a strong arm to protect them. It is not such a very alien idea to some women even today. *The Times* ended its little sermon by hoping that it was not too late to save the marriage. The only redeeming feature of the case was the 'great fixity of affection for his wife' on the part of Fred, the Viscount Dunlo.

Outside the court, Belle received the ovation from the crowd. The case had made her into a heroine. When she came on to the stage of the Empire Theatre that night, the stalls, the pit and the gallery 'rose' to her. From hundreds of throats the words 'Welcome Back!' drowned the orchestra. Enormous floral tributes were handed on to the stage, the corps de ballet thronged round to congratulate her, and the scene shifters and call boys joined in the general rejoicings. The theatre orchestra played a triumphant march to drown the cheers, and the Press representative finally addressed the audience in a 'few well chosen words'.

It was as if Belle had won a victory, not only for herself, but for the whole of her profession. Beauty had defeated the Beast in the best pantomime tradition. Belle's fame sent her salary soaring and she was engaged by Augustus Harris (commonly called 'Druriolanus') and starred in a pantomime with Vesta Tilley, Dan Leno and Whimsical Walker. 'Hearty acclamations awaited the entry of Miss Belle Bilton (Lady Dunlo) in the character of Beauty', wrote *The Times*, 'and the audience joined in the chorus of a pretty little song entitled: "They're after me!"'

The case gave all the papers something to write about, from *The Times* to *Truth*, and the more scurrilous rags, they all had a bad word to say about the Clancarty family. Labouchère described

Wertheimer as 'the only gentleman in the entire crew', a view with which anyone reading the case in detail might be inclined to agree.

An amateur poet wrote a long poem in one of the evening papers, one verse of which ran:

> The Earl of Clancarty should hide his face,
> For beautiful Belle has won her case,
> And the gay young Lord must now regret
> He wanted his marriage to be upset.
> Still everyone can say 'All's Well'
> For Lord Dunlo and Beautiful Belle!

Ten months after he lost the case the Earl of Clancarty died. Belle was on tour and appearing in a show at Plymouth. On 29 May 1891 the news was brought to her that the old man who had tried to ruin her life was no longer able to hurt her. She left the theatre without regret and took the train to London where she joined her husband.

They left for Ireland at once. Fred had inherited Garbally Park, Ballinasloe, County Galway and £12,000 a year. When Belle arrived at her new home, it was as Countess Clancarty – she had left her old life for ever.

It was said that her sweetness of character, and her courage made her much loved amongst her friends, and tenants. Her sportsmanship was also much admired. No doubt she rode straight over the stone walls, and the wide countryside of Galway. Perhaps she rode out with the Blazers. It was admitted, of course, that she could not be received at Court, but Lady Dunlo had been assured that she had the sympathy and personal interest of the Princess of Wales. It was quite understood by the Clancartys that Alexandra was immovable in her resolution 'to ignore women whom her own high principles compelled her to condemn'.

Fred and Belle had twin sons in 1891, and later three other children were born to them.

It is possible to wonder whether, as sometimes Belle looked out from her 'moated grange' across the misty countryside of Galway, she reflected the strange twists of her life. Did she remember, as she visited her tenants as the lady bountiful, the time when she had handled the reins of a smart dog cart driving towards Richmond on a sunny morning? Did she recall with a sigh or a tear, Isidor, the only gentleman in the case?

MARRYING AND GIVING IN MARRIAGE
or
The Sad Tale of the Show Girl and the Hon. James

Victorian melodramas usually had happy endings. The villain was repulsed, the noble hero endured great trials, and the beautiful virtuous blonde heroine was rescued from a fate worse than death. The story of the Hon. James had all the ingredients of a melodrama, except a pure heroine. There were several incipient villains, but none of real calibre. Nor was the central character a hero, he was more of a mug.

Kate Cooke (née Walsh) was an actress of the variety stage when the stage was beginning to shed its raffish image. But while this may have been true of the legitimate theatre, it was not true of Kate Cooke, known amongst the mashers as 'Flash Kate'. Kate's career had started in a circus. Her real name was Walsh, but she had been living with the circus proprietor who was called Cooke, and had assumed his name. Kate may have been a high flyer but she tired of a long run, and after a short time she left Cooke, and the circus. She then joined the chorus of a pantomime in Glasgow where, clad in tights and spangles, she delighted the gentlemen the other side of the footlights. Nor was she reluctant to delight them off stage.

On the strength of her skipping and prancing on the pantomime stage, she felt quite entitled to call herself an actress. From Glasgow she migrated to London where she pursued one, or both, of her professions. She was presumably doing reasonably well, for she had a house in Montpelier Square when she met the Hon. James Henry FitzRoy, son of Lord Charles FitzRoy (educated at Harrow School, sometime an officer in the Rifle Brigade, according to Burke's of the period).

The Hon. James was twenty-two, but from the story which later emerged appears to have been like Bob Brierley in Tom Taylor's *Ticket of Leave Man* 'as green as a leek, soft as new cheese, but steady to ride or drive, and runs in a snaffle'. How he met Kate was not disclosed, but she had been well-known for some time in the

31

more equivocal night haunts of the period, such as the Argyll Rooms and the Holborn Casino. Perhaps, like Bob Brierley, the inexperienced Hon. James had been introduced to 'a thing or two, skittles, billiards, sporting houses, every short cut to the devil, and the bottom of a flat's purse'.

When Tom Taylor wrote his play, with Bob as the wronged hero, he drew an authentic picture of the 1860s, but it is to be suspected that he had, like Dickens, to purify his characters and make them acceptable to his audience. Kate Cooke was no May Edwards, prepared to sing – or starve. Nor would she have accepted a job sewing and housekeeping for an old lady, while chatting in her spare time to her pet canary. If Kate was prepared to chat, it would be to gentlemen, and to some benefit to herself. It seems possible that she had spun a tale of her decline in the world to the Hon. James. For Miss Cooke had told him that her father had been editor of a newspaper. Fathers were easily ruined in Victorian times, and girls had to suffer a touch of ruin themselves in order to keep afloat. It was later to turn out that Kate Cooke was adept at spinning a tale of woe to receptive gentlemen.

Well-known in the night haunts by Tom Browne

So the tempting Miss Cooke enticed the Hon. James into her house in Montpelier Square and, as it was later to transpire, into her bed. He appears to have been a young man of some probity, and not a great deal of sense, for six months later in Worcester he married her. How did Miss Cooke (described as an actress) achieve this desirable end?

The Hon. James had been living with her for six months and he had presumably tested all the sweets of her company, and her bed. But in a period which outwardly believed in the purity of women, it was easy for a young man of family to become enmeshed in the toils of a woman who perhaps pretended to be pregnant, or used her sexual charms as a weapon, not only to dull the senses of a young man, but to get him into such a state of thrall that he seemed to act like a sleepwalker.

Kate had told him her father had been ruined, that she herself was a widow. Suffering from guilt, sexual remorse, tears and tantrums, James probably felt he was saving a poor widow from a life of degradation. What a noble thing saving a woman could seem in an age which believed in heroes being white all through, and heroines suffering from fates worse than death. So the Hon. James, acting honourably, espoused Kate Walsh Smith, widow, in St. Michael's Parish Church in the town of Worcester on 29 May 1871. In view of her widowed state, the bride-to-be preferred the marriage to be secret, and they were married by special licence. The brief ceremony was carried out by a curate of the parish, and the only witnesses were a pew-opener and a solicitor called Froggett.

Froggett was an obliging gentleman. He had advised the wife that a settlement was the thing to have, and the Hon. James made over £10,000, all the money he had in the world, to his wife before he married her. Mr. Froggett kindly arranged the settlement, and the Hon. Mrs. FitzRoy, as Flash Kate had now become, felt that she was settled for life. She had security and a husband, and was no longer dependent on the whims of gentlemen for work and sustenance. Froggett suggested that the money should be put in trust, and he himself very kindly took over the trust fund.

The happy pair set off on a wedding journey. But the marriage bells soon became more than muffled. The kind Mr. Froggett, the helpful Mr. Froggett, made off with the trust fund money, and the happy pair were left with nothing in the kitty. Not at all to the pleasure of Kate Cooke. At this juncture she presumably went back on the stage or, according to the legal reports which put it less delicately, 'resumed her former mode of life', and the unhappy pair lived in a state of disagreement, coming together and separating for the next four years.

The Hon. James now felt himself to be a total outcast. His life had become intolerable, and he had separated from his wife for good. But this seemed to make no difference, his former friends felt that the Hon. James was no longer the kind of man who could be received into good society. Mamas shunned him. He was that pariah of Victorian society, a married man with a wife living, no catch for anyone.

Totally discouraged by the whole thing, the Hon. James sailed for the Antipodes, always a good place for burying oneself away from the eyes of the world. He left England for Australia in 1878.

Once in Australia he seems to have pulled himself together. He found a Government job, and toiled away conscientiously at it until 1882. In this year his uncle died and his father unexpectedly became the Duke of Grafton. As a result of this the Hon. James had become the Earl of Euston. He was still only thirty-three, and still unfortunately married to Kate Cooke.

But the Duke, having succeeded his brother, now set about making some enquiries about Miss Cooke, now supposedly the Countess of Euston. Money was no object to get his son, heir to a great dukedom, free of the toils of a wretched whore who could do nothing but discredit the name of the family.

As it was later put in the court case which ensued (Euston vs. Euston, alias Smith), those who were acting for Lord Euston had been 'put on the alert'. Like Hawkshaw (the Great Detective in Tom Taylor's play), their whiskers were twitching with anticipation. They were not to be proved wrong. Doggedly, and at great length, they pursued their enquiries the length and breadth of the land. Dashing up and down the country from England to Scotland in puffing trains and rattling cabs, they pursued their careful investigations. It was not easy. It was not to anyone's advantage, except Lord Euston's, that the truth should come out. But at last their patience was rewarded.

It was found that at St. Mungo's Catholic Church, Glasgow on 6 July 1863 Kate Cooke (described as an actress) had married a man whose name was George Manby Smith. She, on this occasion, described herself as a spinster, which was not exactly the phrase which Lord Euston's investigators, or his solicitors, would have used. Mr. George Manby Smith was a commercial traveller in some unspecified goods made in Birmingham, and he described himself as a bachelor.

The patient enquirers, who had been put on the alert on behalf of Lord Euston, then sued Lady Euston in a county court. But she came up with a tearful explanation. It was absolutely true that she *had* been married before, but her dear husband George Manby Smith had sailed for Australia in the S.S. *London*, and, alas, the ship had gone down. Mr. George Manby Smith was never seen again by his sorrowing widow, and she swore a Bible oath in open court, that she *was* a widow at the time she had married Lord Euston.

It seemed as if Lord Euston's enquiry agents were baulked. But although baulked they were undeterred.

They went off, and patiently examined the passenger list of the good ship *London* and they found out that a person with the initials G. M. Smith had sailed and gone down in the ship. But they could conclusively prove that although the ill-fated G M. Smith had perished in a watery grave, he was not indeed the G. M. Smith who had married the respondent Lady Euston, alias Smith, but a Mr. George *Maslin* Smith. What was more, by further patient enquiries, they found the widow of Mr. George *Maslin* Smith. She was a Sarah Jane Smith, who had married George Maslin Smith in the month of June 1861. Five years later, presumably suffering from the same financial disadvantages which Lord Euston was later to experience, Mr. Smith (G. M.) sailed for Australia in the ill-fated S.S. *London* and was lost. His widow assured the investigators that she had obtained from the court the necessary papers for the administration of his estate.

The Duke of Grafton and his patient investigators seemed to be successful. Having disposed of the late Mr. George Maslin Smith, all they had to do now was to trace the errant Mr. George *Manby* Smith.

They could not find him, but they did find his old mother, then pushing eighty-three. She gave Lord Euston's solicitors all the information they needed. Her name was Mary Ann Smith, and she had married a George Ashwin Smith in 1827, and produced six children of whom one was George Manby. It was quite true he had sailed for Australia in 1864, although subsequently he had turned up in New Zealand, and he had written to her from Auckland. There, for some reason best known to himself, he was living under the name of Johnson (which name he signed himself to his mother). She also produced a picture of her son. George Manby.

Armed with this evidence the investigators, at some trouble and expense tracked down George Manby and offered to pay his fare and expenses home, should he agree to give evidence for Lord Euston in the case. With some reluctance he eventually agreed. Presumably commercial travelling, even under the name of Johnson, was no more profitable in New Zealand than it had been when he was travelling for a Birmingham firm in Glasgow. But George Manby, being a rolling stone, was quite as prepared to roll home again as to carry on rolling around in the Antipodes. He sailed for

England, prepared to be produced in the court, and to enable Lord Euston to get rid of Kate Cooke.

The investigators had found out that she was living in Watford with a betting man. The ladies behind the footlights, and the gentlemen of the turf seem to have had great attractions for one another in Victorian and Edwardian days. Actresses and horses were both the sport of, if not kings, then heirs to the throne.

The Empire Promenade by Tom Browne

George Manby (all expenses paid), journeyed to Watford, rang the bell of Miss Cooke's house, and quickly identified her as the woman he had so mistakenly married at St. Mungo's Church in the fated year of 1863. He recognised her at once although he had not clapped eyes on her for nearly twenty years. She was obviously not the kind of woman a man could forget. He had been unhappy with her for the whole five months he had been married to her.

Lord Euston (or rather the Duke of Grafton) and his patient investigators were delighted. They had not only traced the marriage certificate, they had found the old mother, and now they had found the errant husband himself. They were home and dry, and could go ahead to free their client from the toils of a designing woman. At this time Lord Euston was only thirty-six, and the Duke was full of hope that, if he were once freed from the terrible Kate, his son could re-make his life.

The case opened on 5 April 1884. Mr. C. Russell Q.C., Mr. Murphy Q.C. and Mr. Lehmann appeared for the petitioner. The respondent was more modest. She was represented by just one Q.C. Mr. Inderwick and by Mr. Montague Williams.

Mr. Russell began in splendid style with a peroration giving the court the benefit of his client's background. Petitioner was the Hon. James Henry FitzRoy, commonly called the Earl of Euston, eldest son of the Duke of Grafton. Admittedly in 1870 his father was only Lord Charles FitzRoy, brother of the Duke of Grafton, and at that time the petitioner himself was only a simple Hon. In 1870 his client had met the respondent, a courtesan. Mr. Russell Q.C. was not disposed to describe her as an actress, whatever profession she may have considered herself to belong to; her Majesty's Counsel put it fairly and squarely that she belonged to the oldest profession. The petitioner made the acquaintance of this courtesan, whose maiden name was Walsh, but who described herself as an actress and called herself 'Kate Cooke'.

The petitioner had 'formed relations' with Miss Cooke, said his Counsel delicately, and had 'visited' her for some months. The marriage took place in Worcester, and on the certificate she described herself as a widow. Counsel then went on to describe the whole sad tale of the gradual decline of the Hon. James, the break-up of the marriage, the disappearance of the helpful Mr. Froggett with the trust money, and the exile of the Hon. James to Australia. He sketched in the story of the two Mr. Smiths, the old mother's tale, and the discovery of the rightful husband of Kate Cooke.

Mr. Murphy Q.C. (for the petitioner) went on to ascertain a few helpful facts.

'How old were you when you met the respondent?'
'Twenty-two.'
'Had you co-habited with the respondent before marriage?'
'Yes.'
'How old did she say she was?'
'Twenty-four.'
It was generally estimated by others that Miss Cooke was known to be 'a good old thirty'.
'Did you ascertain the facts about her age before marriage?'
'No.'
'Did you check the facts about her marriage?'
'No.'

'Did you see her marriage certificate?'

'No.'

'You believed what you had been told?'

'Yes.'

'Yet you settled £10,000 on her *before* marriage.'

'Yes.'

'And then differences arose between you?'

'Yes.'

'Finally you parted?'

'Yes, and I went to Australia in 1875. I returned to England in 1881.'

From the facts so far ascertained, it could be said that Miss Cooke, although a good starter, does not seem to have been a stayer for the course, her marriage with Mr. Manby Smith had lasted only five months, and her 'marriage' with the Hon. James had only been on an intermittent basis.

Mr. Inderwick Q.C. (for the respondent) then cross-examined Lord Euston.

'Was it not true that the petitioner told you that she had been previously married?'

Lord Euston did not reply, and Counsel continued.

'Surely Mr. Froggett, the solicitor who was handling your affairs made some enquiries about the previous marriage?'

'I did see the marriage certificate, but so far as I can recall, it was after my marriage that I received the certificate of my wife's first marriage.'

'Did you know Manby Smith?'

'No. I only ever saw him once in my life and that was when I accompanied him to the – respondent's house so that Smith could identify her.'

Counsel seemed obviously astonished that anyone should be so crass as to marry an alleged widow without making sure that she *was* a widow.

Manby Smith was then produced, and examined by Mr. Russell (for the petitioner).

He told the tale of his going to Australia, and then on to New Zealand.

'What happened when you were in Auckland?'

'A gentleman arrived at my door – he had a letter and a photograph.'

'What was the reason of his visit?'

'He offered me a trip to England – all expenses paid, if I would give evidence of my marriage.'

'You were married?'

'Yes, I married Kate Cooke in July 1863 at St. Mungo's Church, Glasgow.'

'Why did you marry her?'

For a second Mr. Manby Smith looked astonished and then he replied: 'Well, she was living with a man called Cooke, and working in a circus. She was unhappy. The man was unkind to her.'

'Maltreated her?'

'Yes. So I decided to take her away, and – we got married.'

'Were you happy?'

'I can't say we were.'

'How long were you together?'

'Five months.'

'Did you write to your mother from New Zealand – signing yourself Johnson?'

'Yes, I did.'

Mr. Manby Smith could see no reason why he should not sign himself Johnson if he wanted to.

'Is it not true that you had been married before you married Kate Cooke?'

'Certainly. I was married to a Mary Anne Smith.'

'What was her maiden name?'

'Johnson. I married for the first time on 26 June 1862 – but I was separated from my wife after eight months...'

Like Kate Cooke, George Manby Smith did not seem to have been a stayer in the marriage stakes.

'Before I married Kate Cooke, I was told my wife was dead.'

'Who told you?'

'A friend of my first wife in Birmingham.'

'What was the name of the friend?'

'I don't remember.'

'How long was that before you married Kate Cooke?'

'Three months. I never saw my first wife again after I left her.

'Is there the slightest doubt that the woman sitting before you in Court was the Kate Cooke you married in 1863.'

'No.'

When he was cross-examined by the Counsel for the respondent George Manby Smith admitted that he had only seen his wife for a minute, and not a word had been spoken. Presumably Miss Cooke had slammed the door in the face of her two husbands when they had tracked her down.

But Mr. Inderwick suddenly informed the court that his client now had an opportunity of seeing the witness who had just given evidence, and she admitted that he *was* the George Manby Smith with whom she went through a ceremony of marriage in 1863.

So far so good.

At this point the Counsel for the petitioner, in order to prove that the wrong Mr. Smith had perished with the wreck of the good ship *London*, produced Mrs. Sarah Jane Smith.

'Were you married to George Maslin Smith in June of 1861?'

'Yes I was. He left home for Plymouth on January 1st 1866, and sailed in the S.S. *London* for Australia.'

'He was lost with the ship?'

'Yes.'

Counsel paused to let the fact of the widow's grief sink into the minds of the Jury.

'Did you as his widow obtain in this court administration to his estate?'

'I did.'

Mrs. Smith stepped down, and another Mrs. Smith took her place. This time it was George Manby Smith's mother.

Examined by Mr. Russell Q.C. for the petitioner, Mary Ann Smith said she was eighty-three years old.

'You were married?'

'Yes, I was married to George Ashwin Smith in 1827, and I had six children by my marriage.'

'One of these was George Manby Smith?'

'Yes.'

'Did he leave this country for Australia?'

'Yes, and then he went to New Zealand. I had a letter from him from Auckland. He signed himself George Johnson.'

The old lady handed some letters and a photograph of her son to the petitioner's solicitor for purposes of identification. That concluded the case for Lord Euston. It looked as if his father had managed to un-mesh him from Kate Cooke.

Mr. Montague Williams for Kate Cooke then rose. He had another two witnesses to examine. There was a rustling in the Court and an elderly man took the oath.

'Your name is William Henry Johnson?'

'Yes.'

'You had a sister?'

'Yes. Her name was Mary Anne Johnson, and she was married to a man called William Smith.'

'William Smith is dead.'

'Yes, he died in January of 1853.'

'Were there any children of this marriage?'

'Yes. Four.'

'What happened after your sister was widowed?'

'She came to live with me bringing three children with her. But in

40

1861 she returned to Birmingham and lived there. I went down to Birmingham in the autumn of 1862 and found that she had in her house a George Manby Smith.'

'The same man who has been examined today?'

'Yes. I found out that this man had married my sister.'

'What date was that?'

'They were married on June 26th 1862.'

It would appear that Mr. Johnson did not approve of the marriage because he did not see his sister again until 1866.

'When did you see your sister again?'

'I received a communication to the effect that my sister, Mrs. George Manby Smith was dangerously ill at Edgbaston near Birmingham. That was in November of 1866.'

'You went down?'

'Yes. I went down with my sister Phillis from London.'

'And how was your sister?'

'We found her in a very bad state, a very bad state indeed.'

'She died?'

'Yes. She died on June 9th 1867.'

This was, unfortunately for Lord Euston, nearly four years after the marriage of George Manby Smith and Kate Cooke.

'Were you present at the death?'

'Yes.'

'Did you register the death?'

'Yes, I went with my sister Phillis and we registered the death together.'

'That is the certificate which is now in court?'

'Yes.'

Mr. Russell, Q.C. (for the petitioner) had no questions to ask the witness.

Mr. Johnson stepped down, and his sister Phillis was called.

'You are Phillis Johnson?'

'Yes,'

'Do you corroborate the testimony of the last witness that your sister was alive up to 9 June 1867?'

'Yes. I was at her deathbed.'

At this point the case for the petitioner, Lord Euston, collapsed.

Mr. Russell Q.C. said, 'I cannot controvert the testimony of the last two witnesses.'

The President then summarised the complications of the marrying and giving in marriage.

'It is now admitted that the George Manby Smith whom we have seen in the box is the person who was lawfully married to Mary Anne Smith, widow on 26 June 1862. He not then being in a position to contract a lawful marriage because of his wife Mary Anne Smith being alive. Kate Walsh was then free to marry because she was not lawfully married to George Manby Smith because he had a wife alive.'

The Jury at once found that George Manby Smith was legally married to Mary Anne Smith on 26 June 1862, that Kate Walsh was *not* lawfully married to the said George Manby Smith on 6 July 1863, that the said George Manby Smith was alive on 29 May 1871, and that the petitioner and the respondent *were* legally married on 29 May 1871.

The President: 'This is a finding for the respondent, and the petition is dismissed – with costs.'

It is easy to imagine the triumphant flash of victory in the eyes of Kate Cooke as she looked across the court towards her husband, who had hoped to prove that he was not.

He walked through the gloomy corridors out into the street, with little future before him. He could not marry again, and he did not live in an age which regarded a divorced man with any degree of pleasure. An indiscretion of a youth of twenty-two had ruined the life of a man in his thirties.

The Times voted it the most extraordinary case that had ever been tried in the Divorce Court. 'Had such a tale as that unfolded in court formed the plot of a novel or a play, the author would have been reproved for sinning against the probabilities and straining after effects. . . The imagination of few novelists would be equal to conceiving a medley and tangle of domestic relations similar to that exhibited in this story of a mésalliance.'

Poor Lord Euston's plight evoked some sympathy, but one of the cheaper Sunday papers took the chance of inveighing against the upper classes. 'Even a modicum of correct conduct is not always observable among our aristocrats. Noblesse Oblige had not prevented the Earl of Euston (the future Duke of Grafton) from bringing a trumped-up charge of bigamy against his Countess and attempting to prevent her enjoying the rank and position to which she is fully entitled. We are shocked that such an attempt should have been made.' It was disgraceful, aristocrats could not play fast and loose with 'the standards of those who do not happen to be born in the purple.'

Poor James FitzRoy incurred the disability of marrying a courtesan, and at the same time seemed to merit the censure of the respectable lower middle classes enjoying the discomforture of a gilded aristocrat, as they masticated their bacon and eggs behind their lace curtains.

The Earl of Euston never married again. No doubt he had had

enough of marrying and giving in marriage. It is to be hoped that he found some *femme complaisante* to comfort his solitude, even if the mores of the times did not countenance open co-habitation.

Kate Cooke died in 1903. The Earl of Euston in 1912. The Old Duke of Grafton lived on until he was over ninety, and so the unfortunate James, the chief sufferer in the trial, never achieved either legitimate heirs – or his dukedom.

THE PRINCE AND THE COLUMBINE

💟💟💟💟💟💟💟💟💟💟💟💟💟💟💟💟💟💟💟💟💟💟💟💟💟💟

When Prince George, eldest son of the Duke of Cambridge, was born in the Palace at Hanover, he was a very important baby indeed. He was third in line to succeed to the British throne and become King. His two uncles George IV and William IV were devoid of legitimate offspring, and anything could – with luck – happen to the pregnant Duchess of Kent.

The unfortunate and sudden death of the Princess Charlotte in childbed caused a flurry of marriages amongst the libertine brothers of George IV. Never was there such a discarding of old mistresses, a dealing out of minor German princesses, or such a conceiving of legitimate heirs. Prince George was the fruit of one of these marriages. His father, the fourth son of George III, Adolphus, Duke of Cambridge, drew Augusta, daughter of the Landgrave Frederick of Hesse-Cassel, out of the pack. The wedding had taken place at Cassel on 7 May 1818, and to make surety doubly sure, the happy couple were married again in England. After the two marriages, the Duke with his Duchess returned to Hanover, where eleven months later in March of 1819 their son, George, was born.

So important was the birth that it was attended and verified by H.R.H. The Duke of Clarence, the Rt. Hon. Earl of Mayo, and the Rt. Hon. George Henry Rose (Envoy Extraordinary and Minister Plenipotentiary at the Court of Berlin). They were there to certify that no live baby in a warming-pan was substituted for a stillborn child. It was a very serious business when Prince George first saw the light of day.

The Duke of Clarence, the Earl of Mayo, and the Ambassador sealed a solemn document to the effect that her Royal Highness was confined in her bedroom up one pair of stairs, and that although the midwives had to have free access from the dressing-room, the three gentlemen not only sealed their document, but they also sealed the dressing-room door.

His Royal Highness the Duke of Cambridge ... locked the door and gave the key of it to the said Right Honourable George Henry Rose, so that no communication with the bedroom could take place from without, but under Our eyes, we remaining in the room adjoining to the bedroom, and through which all persons entering that bedroom must pass; that sharp labor continued until ten minutes past two o'clock of the morning aforesaid, when Her Royal Highness the Duchess of Cambridge was safely delivered of a male child, whose sex we determined by actual inspection.

The three gentlemen opined that the child appeared to be healthy and well-grown. He was christened on 22 May 1819 with all due ceremonies of the rites of the established Church of England. Neither being well-grown, nor C. of E. did Prince George any permanent good, because two months later the Duchess of Kent produced Princess Victoria, who turned out to be very healthy herself, no doubt much to the chagrin of the family at Hanover. But they had not given up hope.

In 1830 his parents sent Prince George over to England. Should anything unfortunately happen to the Princess Victoria, they reflected, he would be King of England, and it was as well to be prepared. He was eleven years old, and took up residence with William IV and his Queen Adelaide, who both became very fond of him. He proved to be a solemn humourless boy, and was constantly (admittedly under the supervision of his tutor) writing reproving pieces to himself in his diary. '7 January 1832. I am sorry to say . . . I showed some signs of cowardice on horseback.'

'14 April 1834. Behaved very ill yesterday morning about bathing, really quite like a baby.'

He seems to have met the Princess Victoria from time to time at family parties. 'A large party, among others the Duchess of Kent and Princess Victoria, who has a nice countenance and is greatly improved.'

It was apparently the family plan that, if Victoria were not carried off by some fell disease, then George, if not succeeding, could at least marry her. George had his faults, as he was the first to admit. 'My most glairing [sic] fault now is that I desire to argue with everybody, and then after all I am generally in the wrong.' But King William and his Queen were still full of hope that the cousins would marry. To celebrate Princess Victoria's fourteenth birthday they gave a ball at St. James's Palace. The Princess opened the ball by dancing with George. But 'poor George', as Queen Victoria was later to call him, does not seem to have been much of a social success, as he himself sadly noted: 'Yesterday was the King's birthday – a very full drawing room (1,400 persons) Mr. Wood [his tutor] gave me a hint about behaving better in society and speaking to people in a more pleasing manner.'

The following year he does not seem to have made much progress:

> I am sorry to say I behaved very ill indeed on several occasions, and was very unkind in my language to dear Mr. Wood. I got so violent ... that I was obliged to leave the room, and if I do not behave well during the week I am not to hunt. The Houses of Parliament are entirely burnt down. . . . The King and Queen went to see the ruins.

In August of 1835 he was confirmed and noted that it 'went off remarkably well', and in the same month he was made a Knight of the Garter. The latter event seems to have impressed the Prince more. 'I am delighted to say that yesterday [the Garter Ceremony] went off remarkably well. . . . The King has been kind enough to give me a most beautiful set of the Order. Two stars, and two splendid Georges, besides what I have got from the Lord Chamberlain's office.' The ceremony had not only turned out well, but profitable.

The following spring when George was seventeen, Queen Adelaide consulted the Duke of Wellington as to the course which the Prince's further education should follow. Writing in 1836, the Duke's opinion was that 'His Royal Highness is in that position as that it may happen to be called upon to exert all the energies of his mind, at a very early period of his life.' No one was giving up hope of the elevation of the Prince to the state of Consort. The Duke felt that the study of the theory of the military profession 'is not incompatible with other studies'. The main thing was 'to form his mind, his principles and his judgement'.

The Army was decided upon as his career. It was much to the Prince's liking, for he had been given the patent of Colonel *en second* of the Guard Jäger Regiment of the Hanovarian Army when he was eight years old. Consequently, accompanied by his military Governor, Colonel Cornwall (of the Coldstream Guards), he went back to Hanover and was rapidly promoted from private to officer. At only seventeen, he was delighted with his new role of officer. 'I mounted my first Guard at the Palace at Hanover. Lieutenant Baring was on Guard with me. I must confess it was one of the happiest days of my life, for I, for the first time, felt as if I was really a soldier.'

Just to prove it, the Prince marched his men up the avenue

leading to the summer Palace of the Duke and Duchess – so that his mother and sister could see him, splendidly attired, giving orders to his men. The passions for marching, countermarching, and the niceties of uniform were to last him, with equal enthusiasm, all his life. As he grew older he added the length, or absence, of moustachios to these other enthusiasms.

In 1837, when William IV died, and Victoria became Queen, it was a double blow for the Cambridge family. A woman could not succeed to the throne of Hanover. The Prince wrote:

> The death of our poor dear King, besides the sorrow we all feel for his personal loss, is in another way a most severe blow to us all, particularly to my own family. . . . My uncle the Duke of Cumberland has now become the king of that country. My father is therefore removed from the Government of the country where he has lived for these 24 years and where we have all been born.

It was decided that the whole troop of the Cambridge family should live in England. Hopes were presumably still running high on George's chances with the Queen.

On 10 May 1838 the Prince opened the Coronation Ball by dancing with the young Queen. George wrote, 'I thought she danced really very nicely, and seemed to be very much amused.' 'The rooms looked remarkably well, the people were uncommonly well dressed, and very smart, both Ladies and Gentlemen, but more particularly the former, of which there were a great many pretty ones.'

In his diaries in whatever country he travelled the Prince often commented on the looks of the women. Good looks obviously affected him greatly. Some men and women find it impossible to be drawn to ugly people however admirable their characters, and this was obviously a trait in George's nature which was to affect his later conduct. On 17 May he wrote, 'Today was appointed the young Queen's birthday. . . . I went to the Drawing Room, a very large one, 2,200 people being there, among whom, however, there was a considerable collection of ugly ones.'

On the 28th of the next month the Queen was crowned, although George noted in his diary that she 'looked less well than usual'. It was a point of view which the young Queen had held about Prince George for some considerable time, and in 1839 she proved it by becoming engaged to Prince Albert.

'Poor George' had spent part of 1838, and most of 1839, travelling around the Mediterranean being instructed in military matters, commenting on the wretchedness of foreign troops, and the handsome looks of foreign women. When he returned to England at the end of 1839 the Queen's engagement was official. George had noted in his diary some years before: 'What a very disagreeable thing it must be to be a king! May I never be one.' His fervent prayer had been answered in full measure. In 1840 the Queen married Albert, and quickly produced two children, putting an end to the hopes of the Cambridge family.

About the time of Victoria's marriage, Prince George went to the pantomime, not an historical event in itself. But in the thirties and forties of the last century pantomime had a glitter and excitement which lifted it above the everyday life of the grey streets. Here in the darkness, as the gaslit transformation scenes unfolded, could be seen troupes of coryphées in their diaphanous dresses, beautiful girls dressed in lush Eastern costumes, thinly disguised as gentlemen, and underneath their transparent Turkish knee length trousers could be seen that wonder of the age – the female leg, a delight not to be glimpsed anywhere else in public.

It was admitted that the Prince was not much of a theatre-goer, but pantomime was all part of the general family fun of Christmas, and to the pantomime, Prince George duly went. And there for the first time he set eyes on Miss Louisa Fairbrother.

Louisa was the daughter of a printer who had much objected to his beautiful daughter dancing in public on the stage, but she had a will of her own, and managed to get into the pantomime at Drury Lane. She was not only beautiful, but had an elegant figure, and a charming ladylike presence. None of this seemed to have entranced one of her critics. Her first appearance on 27 December was marked by lack of journalistic enthusiasm. 'Miss Fairbrother's Columbine would require *very* little search to find an equal.' The same critic visited the show some time later in the same season, and had not altered his opinion either about her, or the show. 'The view of London was at a standstill for a full five minutes while Gravesend, and Rochester, came tumbling on to it, leaving the unlucky metropolis covered with creases.' Undeterred by her bad notices, the determined Louisa joined Mr. and Mrs. Keeley at the Lyceum where she continued to play Columbine, and to dance in her dainty skirts across the stage.

Prince George fell immediately and desperately in love with her. There was nothing to deter him. Victoria was safely married, and all set to produce a number of children, who would debar him for ever from the throne of England. His official biographer stated: 'On matrimony as on other matter, from his very early days, His Royal Highness's views were clear, precise, and not easily subject to change. He held that marriage without *love* was destined to end in

48

Miss Fairbrother as Columbine

failure and disaster and that a union "by arrangement" was a thing to be feared and detested.' Whether he came by his view from choice, or disappointment, remains unclear. There was also the matter of his predilection for good-looking women. Beauty was in fairly short supply among German princesses, and beauty, handsome clothes, and symmetry affected the Prince greatly. It could be either the beauty of women, or the symmetry of a Scottish regiment swinging along to their regimental band. Early in his life he had given up his piano and organ playing as these were considered not to be manly occupations, and now only the beauty of women and the beauty of discipline remained aesthetically satisfying to him.

The fact was that as a result of falling in love with his Columbine he was pushed into doing the only dashing thing he was ever to do in his life. He married, with benefit of clergy, but without benefit of the Queen's permission. The family-conscious Queen, with her endless numbers of petty royal German relatives – all burdened with marriageable daughters – would never have given her permission for Prince George, her cousin, to marry into the pantomime, and form an alliance with a Columbine.

Prince George married his Columbine at St. John's Church, Clerkenwell, and described himself as 'George William Cambridge, Gent. of St. Paul's, Dartford'.

There is on the part of the Duke's biographers some slight discrepancy about dates. The Duke himself in later life talked of 'my companion of 50 years', which would mean he met his Louisa about 1840. The most likely date for the marriage would seem to be 1842, for although Louisa was dancing during that year, her first son was born in 1843. It was also the year in which Prince George was packed off on military duties to the Ionian Islands for two years.

In 1844, Louisa had gone back to the theatre, though not without mishaps. In October of that year, she played in a piece called *Seven Castles* where, by waving her fairy wand she caused 'the curtain to be taken up by mistake, revealing Mr. Keeley casually picking wigs from the stage, Mrs. Keeley giving directions to an elderly female in plain private attire carrying a bundle of clothes. Miss Farebrother [sic] whose potent wand had brought about the change in the last tableau was flying before a scene, which some men were hurrying – like a huge covered clothes horse – across the stage.'

In the same year, Louisa played the fair ward Isabel in a comedietta called *Watch and Ward*, in which she was in love – rather appropriately – with a dashing young officer, and her romance was being thwarted by her guardian the old Baron de Brissac. Later in the Christmas pantomime she played Aladdin. In this part she wore a splendid costume of glittering scarlet bodice, an embroidered zouave, a short thigh length tulle skirt, some knee length tulle trousers of vaguely oriental design, topped off with a feathered hat, a black wig, and a small moustache and imperial beard, a costume hardly likely to appeal either to Queen Victoria, or Prince Albert.

The married lovers must have felt that they had been parted for ever. The Sub-Dean of His Majesty's Chapels Royal and Canon of Windsor admitted, when writing the Prince's biography, that the diaries for the years from 1840 to 1849 were missing. It was unfortunate, he felt, for the Prince must have had much to say about his travels. He also probably had much to say about his love for Louisa. 1840 to 1849 were the years in which he wooed and won her, and fathered his three sons.

The Prince came back to England briefly in 1845, and his second son was born in 1846. By that time he had been packed off again to Ireland, although a brief leave produced a third son in 1847. The gaps in his diaries were made up by his biographer by the publication of some of his letters. On going back to Dublin from leave, he wrote to his mother:

It was certainly with a very heavy heart that I parted from you the other day, but be assured I come here with good courage and will do my very utmost to show they may have confidence in me. All I ask in return is that they also may show some wish to fulfil my wishes.

Was this a reference to his marriage?

On his return to Dublin, he found it sad and dull. He was occupied in the mornings but 'the solitary evenings one does not know what to do with oneself'. He brooded that surely 'an opening may be found for me in a post that will call me to England. Such is my aim and wish.' He thought of his Louisa in London with her three baby sons growing up around her, and he so far away.

The Queen and Prince Albert made an official visit to Ireland in 1849. They seemed, wrote the Prince, very pleased with everything he had done. The Queen presented him with the Order of St. Patrick, and Prince Albert commented on 'my military knowledge which is a fresh proof that he is kindly disposed towards me'. But neither of them mentioned bringing poor George back to London. Perhaps they had yet another German princess in view for him.

In 1850 George's father died, he became Duke of Cambridge, and returned to England. His father's death affected him greatly, George was not only a devoted and faithful husband, but a devoted and faithful son. 'I have lost a father and the best friend I had on earth.' Possibly George's father had been sympathetic over his marriage, and understood his love for Louisa. In a sense, some of the Prince's troubles had been resolved by the death of the Duke. Parliament (with a little nudging from the Queen) fixed his income at £12,000 a year, and he took his place in the House of Lords. The Queen wrote that she 'rejoiced to be of use to you on this occasion. . . . You have true friends in both of us who entertain truly Geschwisterliche Gefühle toward you.' Some family difficulties had been resolved, although the family had not accepted George's so-called 'morganatic marriage'.

He set himself up in bachelor rooms in St. James's Palace, and only a short walk or drive away, was his dear Louisa always ready with his slippers, his children, and a warm fireside in Queen Street, Mayfair. Officially the Duke of Cambridge was a bachelor and became in great demand for making speeches, opening things, launching things, and commenting on things at dinners.

For reasons of security and economy Mrs. Fitzgeorge, as Louisa came to be known, had none but female servants. It is well known to intelligence officers that women keep secrets better than men, and

Mrs. Fitzgeorge's servants kept hers. So she lived her life in her comfortable home providing poor George with all the home comforts he needed when he was able to snatch a few delightful hours away from his wearying official business. Mrs. Fitzgeorge never became a Royal Highness or a Duchess, but she kept her dignity. When his Royal Highness slipped round from St. James's Palace to his home in Queen Street, he slipped out of his trappings as a Royal Highness and he became Mr. Fitzgeorge, his Louisa insisted on that. If she was Mrs. Fitzgeorge, it was fitting he should be Mr. Fitzgeorge.

In September of 1852, the Duke of Wellington, George's sponsor and mentor died. George heard the rumour, and prudently walked up to Apsley House to make sure it was true. It was, and he was appointed to be in charge of the troops. On 18 November he wrote in his diary. 'This is the great day appointed for the Duke's funeral. Though most unpromising in the morning, it turned out to be a most beautiful day. Up and dressed by 6.15 and out by a quarter before 7. I had the entire command and responsibility as regarded the troops. Everything went off to perfection.' Precision, com-

My beloved Louisa. From a painting by Joy

H.R.H. George, Duke of Cambridge, K.G. From a painting by Winterhalter

mand and discipline, that was what the Duke had expected, and George was determined to see that he received his due on his last journey.

In 1854 the Crimean War broke out, and the Duke of Cambridge set off for the front by a somewhat roundabout way via Paris to see the Emperor of the French and wrote that the Empress was decidedly handsome, and then to Leipzig to try to persuade the Germans to join in. He then visited Vienna arriving in time for the young Emperor's marriage, and noted his bride was also decidedly handsome. The only unfortunate note was that George was unable to persuade either Germans or Austrians to join in the war. By the time he joined his regiment in camp in Varna disorganisation was already beginning, and by July cholera had broken out. By August the disease was spreading, and had attacked the Navy as well as the French armies. But eventually George set sail and landed in the Crimea.

He fought at Alma, and had his horse shot from under him at Inkerman, his life being saved by a wounded Russian.

A Captain Peel gave an account of the Duke's escape:

On our way we passed through many killed and wounded – English and Russian. A Russian Officer who was badly wounded, cried 'Water! Give me water to drink!' I gave him some from my flask and he said 'Tell your people to come out of that battery, they are going to be surrounded.' We saw through our field glasses through the mist the Irkutsky Regiment. . . . this intelligence was conveyed to H.R.H. The Duke of Cambridge who immediately ordered the men to fall in, put the Colours in the midst and made a rush with fixed bayonets at the Irkutsky Regiment which was coming down the hillside, and cut their way through the fire. The Duke of Cambridge rode past the enemy with his A.D.C. Major Macdonald but not unscathed for he was hurt by a ball which grazed his arm and his charger was shot under him. . . . So the Russian Officer's important and timely information saved the Duke of Cambridge, the handful of soldiery, and the Colours of the Grenadier Guards.

But the Army had lost 14,000 out of 24,000 men, and many of those who remained were sick or dying. The Duke himself was sick with fever and taken on board a ship. But his troubles were not over, the ships lying in harbour were struck by a storm, and in danger of being dashed to pieces on the rocks, then the ship where he lay sick was struck by a thunderbolt. 'This cleared the atmosphere', wrote the Duke, 'and the wind gradually went down.'

The Duke was eventually sent on sick leave to Constantinople. He noted that all the letters he received from England urged him to go back to the Crimea. Albert wrote how deeply he envied him being in it all, and noted that he, Albert, had had fifty sealskin coats made to present to the officers of his regiment. The Queen sent news of her whole household knitting furiously. But in January the Duke had decided on the advice of Lord Stratford to go to Malta. He was still sickly and suffering from the ague. It was rumoured that his Louisa went out to nurse him. He arrived in Malta on 6 January, and on the ship with him were many other sick and wounded men from the battlefields. He took up his quarters in 'a nice family hotel'. Did his Louisa await him there to cherish him back to health?

On 21st he sailed for England and arrived at Dover on 30th. 'Reached town at 6, and drove at once to St. James's, where I found my dearest Mother and Mary, . . . and then went to my dearest Aunt Gloucester.' He added, 'Early home, and thankful to God for having once again restored me to my dear family and friends.' Away from the battles and the sickness he still thought of the sufferings of

54

his dear comrades. 'I am a poor creature, but certainly much better for the journey, and for the society of my family and friends, so that I doubt not a very short time will set me all to rights again.'

He was with his Louisa, and his sons were already growing up – eleven, eight and seven. It was good to be home in Queen Street, as Mr. Fitzgeorge, after so many dangers overcome. The Duke was seldom to be separated from his Louisa again except for a few weeks. In 1855 he was offered the Governorship of Gibraltar, 'I have thought it advisable for many reasons to decline.' He preferred his marriage to serving abroad. He was to devote the rest of his life to public ceremonial and private domesticity.

The calm tenor of his way was broken by some ceremonial abroad. He went to Paris to present the Crimean Medals to the French veterans of that war. 'Nothing could have gone off better and the greatest enthusiasm pervaded the troops.' He was in Council with the Emperor and discussed the preliminaries for peace.

He returned to England and on 29 February gave a dinner party at St. James's which the Queen attended. 'The dinner passed off satisfactorily and well, with the exception of the upsetting of a dish of fish over the Queen.'

But the Peace Treaty was concluded and peace was signed on 30 March 1856. He had fought in the war and was of diplomatic help in concluding the peace 'conveying to the Emperor that the feeling of the Country here (in France) is most decidedly for Peace. This should be known in England.'

The Duke had noted in the same year that it had been decided that the post of Commander-in-Chief should 'stay as it is'. This was to have some bearing on his future. In July 1856, while there was a great deal of inspecting and marching of troops at Aldershot, Lord Hardinge, Commander-in-Chief of the Army, had a stroke while talking to the Queen and Prince Albert. A week later Hardinge resigned and the Cabinet recommended His Royal Highness the Duke of Cambridge to succeed him.

He wrote to his mother: 'So it is all settled and I am Commander-in-Chief. I heard from Lord Palmerston, and the Queen sent for me to come to her this evening and announced it to me in the presence of Albert. She was very much moved and I saw it touched her very nearly, but she was exceedingly gracious and friendly.' The Duke wrote that, 'it is a tremendous undertaking, but yet I am quite of good courage, for all are *for* me.'

He made a note in his diary: 'Thus I am placed in the proudest military position any subject could be placed in. It is an onerous one, but I will do my best to do myself credit.'

He had succeeded at last to the post of his hero and mentor the Duke of Wellington. He was also to succeed to many of the Duke's opinions. In 1881 the question of the sale of Commissions and the reform of the Army came up: 'It has been decided to make great changes in the Army in spite of my earnest remonstrances, but I have not succeeded in preventing them, which I greatly deplore.' If the sale of Commissions were to be abolished who knows what kind of people would get into the Army? There should be no damned nonsense of merit about promotion. Family tradition, courage and discipline were all that were needed. The Duke of Cambridge was born four years after the Iron Duke's great battle, but in his opinions he bore many resemblances to the veteran portrayed by Irving in *A Story of Waterloo*. Corporal Brewster constantly remarked, with many a bronchitic wheeze: 'It would never 'ave done for the Dook.' A sentiment echoed by George, Duke of Cambridge.

The Duke liked being Commander-in-Chief and he remained Commander-in-Chief from 1856 until 1895, although the last years were years of conflict about the post. In 1890 George noted: 'Saw Mr. Stanhope and had a long talk to him about the Report of the Royal Commission, which recommended the prospective abolition of the Commander-in-Chief – a most deplorable recommendation!' The Duke was seventy-one, and it was felt that it was high time he retired, but the skirmishing between the Queen and the Duke against the government went on until 1895, when the post was finally abolished, which was one way of achieving the Duke's retirement.

In 1857 the year after he had been made Commander-in-Chief his aunt Mary, Duchess of Gloucester, the sister of his father, died. The Duchess had no children, and she left her property including Gloucester House to George, her dear nephew. This inheritance presented George with some problems. He was quite happy in his bachelor rooms in St. James's and his home in Queen Street with Louisa. What did he want with a large house? He was not only wretched at the loss of his aunt: 'We went and took a last look at that dear face we loved so well', but he did not want to move. On the other hand it might seem odd and cause comment if he did not move into Gloucester House. On looking over it, he wrote: 'It is certainly a very fine house, but I'm afraid would never be comfortable to me as a *man*.' George's tastes were simple – he liked a pleasant, good-looking wife, and a cosy home. Splendour, except in the military and ceremonial sense, was not for him. But, by 1860 he had decided to move in. 'Today alas! I leave my dear apartment at St. James's in order to remove to Gloucester House. I confess I am very low and miserable about it, but it must be done and there is no help for it. For

The Duke as Commander-in-Chief (post abolished 1895)

19 years I have lived in these dear rooms, and many are the happy hours I have spent there.'

When Prince Albert died, and the Queen retired into grieving widowhood, poor George had more and more ceremonial heaped upon him. Albert's second Great International Exhibition caused a flurry of entertaining of foreign delegations, and welcoming of foreign royalties. Military reviews, weddings, christenings, small and large luncheons, small and large dinners, speeches, short and long, valedictory and welcoming, all fell to George's lot. And above all funerals. Judging by his diary the Duke seems to have been used as a specialist in funerals, both family and public. Considering his very tender heart this was hard on him. But, of course, Victoria was in no state to be upset by funerals, and was even inclined to grieve at weddings, so it was only seemly that George should shoulder most of the official grief.

Nothing was too small or too large for George's official attendance. 'Opening of a People's Park at Crewe. Special train placed at my disposal by the Directors of North Western Railway.' A month later he went to the German Chapel for the official funeral service for the Emperor Frederick, Victoria's son-in-law. 'The results of his early demise can only be contemplated with the gravest anxiety.' The Duke, although misguided in many of his opinions, was right in his fears. It was only 1888 when he wrote those words, but his forebodings were fulfilled by the war in 1914.

On and on, over the years more and more official business was laid on the Duke. In his diary, he noted without complaint, occasional bouts of gout, but by and large he continued healthy and dutiful.

In 1890, when he was nearly seventy-one, Louisa died.

Sunday, 12 January. My beloved wife breathed her last calmly, peacefully, softly at about 4 of this morning ... all her children as well as myself, the nurse, dear Rowley and the female servants were surrounding the deathbed, a peaceful gathering of devotedly mourning and affectionate hearts. ... My beloved one lay lovely in death still amongst us. Her countenance was beautiful, quite young to look at, though 74 in actual age. ... She was so good and kind and affectionate and true and generous-hearted and my little home of 50 years with my beloved Louisa is now come to an end.

He announced the news to the Queen, and received an affectionate message from her. 'It would have been such a joy to my beloved one had she known the fact.'

Louisa was buried wearing the bracelet he had given her, and was laid to rest at Kensal Green, 'behind the Chapel in a piece of ground I bought for myself some years ago, and where I propose to be laid myself by her dear side.'

On 23 January he went to Queen Street 'to take affectionate leave of the dear old house where I have spent so many many happy years of my life with my beloved wife.' George lived on for another fourteen years, but he never ceased to love and to regret her. When in France he wrote: 'How I miss her! It is indescribable and nothing more so at this moment when absent than not hearing from, or writing to her daily as has always been our habit since we first met.'

He had seen his Columbine at the pantomime, fallen in love with her, overcome all obstacles, and remained faithful unto death.

MARIE TEMPEST
or
Becky, a Rogue in Porcelain

Marie Tempest's rise to fame and social eminence is symptomatic of the lives of many actresses of her age. She was born to obscurity, but married the grandson of a duke, and dominated the West End theatre for more than fifty years.

She was not beautiful. Her nose was retroussé, her eyes were small and quick, but they were smiling, coquettish eyes. Her public always expected her to be archly tempting. If she had to weep, it must be daintily into a small lace handkerchief, perhaps only as a ruse to get her man, for she must always remain mistress of the situation. With her swift sweeping walk, she commanded the stage from the moment she made her entrance. She was a queen of light comedy which she had made into her own art form, for she seemed born to be without melancholy. She was described as a Puck in petticoats and an Ariel in stockings. Yet she came from nowhere, and inherited nothing except her native wit.

Marie Tempest was born on 15 July 1864 – Mary Susan Etherington. Her father was a stationer in a small way of business in Wigmore Stree. He was the illegitimate son of Sarah Etherington, daughter of Thomas Etherington, a blacksmith who plied his trade in Midhurst in Sussex. It was generally believed that Mary Susan's father, Edwin, was the son of a gentleman of good family, and a soldier by profession.

In Miss Tempest's official biography she spoke to her biographer Hector Bolitho, of a 'tall blond soldier', her mysterious guardian, whom she was accustomed to visit in Baker Street, not far from where her father carried on his humble trade purveying writing paper to the nobility and gentry. According to her account, this guardian lived in some style with a personal valet. If this guardian were, in fact, her grandfather, he had obviously behaved well by his son, setting him up in business, and seeing that he did not starve.

Mary Susan (later to become Dame Marie Tempest) appears to have appliqued a much better story to her antecedents at this point. According to her account her father drank, and her mother left him taking her two sisters to Canada. Even if the story of her father's drunkenness were true, he was still in his small way of business in Wigmore Street from 1860 until 1878 when Mary Susan was fourteen, and quite able to take in the circumstances of her undistinguished family. But the Victorians, living in an age of many parvenus, were always disposed to hide their origins when they were climbing to a higher social plane. It is difficult for our contemporaries to understand this trait. Current politicians, and even actresses, are given to boasting of their humble, if not sordid origins. They demote their ancestors, their grandparents, and even their parents. The manager of a mine becomes a miner, and the owner of a chain of grocery stores a 'storekeeper', as if he were humping sacks of sugar from lorry to warehouse. It is unfashionable to be genteel. People of Miss Tempest's generation were ever conscious of the virtues of gentility, and Miss Tempest was to be no exception.

Marie Tempest. 'A star in every sense of the word' (Noël Coward)

Her grandmother Etherington had married a servant, William Marriage, who had become a yeoman (or caretaker) of the Chapel Royal. This did not seem to be at all suitable to Miss Tempest, then living in a grand house near Regent's Park. She stuck to a few facts when she chatted to her biographer, but preferred to give the impression that her grandmother was an elegant, but retired, kept lady who lived in a very grand house in Whitehall. She painted a picture of her grandmother's cupboards full of expensive dresses. She described the old lady attending church at the Chapel Royal in her rustling silks, chatting in an intimate way with Mr. and Mrs. Gladstone. She herself, a pretty child, had been petted at luncheon parties by Mrs. Charles Tennant, and Sir Charles Dilke. Joseph Chamberlain had patted her on the head. None of these flights of Miss Tempest's imagination seems likely.

It is possible that her grandmother did attend church at the Chapel Royal, but only because her husband was caretaker there. It is also possible she had a silk dress, no doubt a present from some grand lady's wardrobe. Her grandmother could have known some of these notabilities, but only as a result of her husband's humble position. Whether Lady Susan Vane-Tempest, from whom Miss Tempest took her stage name, was in truth her godmother is also in doubt. Sometimes very grand ladies obliged upper servants by standing in as godmother, and giving the child a good send-off and a coral necklace. It was an age which specialised in such condescending gestures.

One true fact emerges from this farrago of romance. Mary Susan Etherington did receive a good education. She was sent first to school at Midhurst, and subsequently to a convent in Belgium at Thildonck. Belgium provided a cheap but excellent training for girls in Victorian times. Ruined families sent their daughters to be educated there; by-blows of aristocratic sons were packed over to the other side of the channel where they would not be so noticeable. There was a plentiful supply of nuns in those far-off days; often the daughters of ruined gentlefolk themselves, they were adept at turning the sow's ears of the lower middle classes into the semblance of the silk purses of the aristocracy. Les Bonnes Ursulines not only taught Mary Susan excellent French, but they taught her to be be a lady. Subsequently she was sent to a private school in Paris, and by the age of sixteen, she could speak and write fluent French, had an excellent accent, and had acquired the appearance and polish of a lady.

It is to be presumed that the tall, blond soldier with his impressive 'Jeeves', who lived in Baker Street, Mary Susan's 'guardian', had paid for her education. He went on paying. She showed some talent for singing and was enrolled at the Royal Academy of Music to study under Manuel Garcia, the most distinguished singing teacher of his age. Garcia had taught Jenny Lind at the Paris Conservatoire before coming to London in 1848. Humble though her origins, Mary Susan was already a long way from the background of the brawny blacksmith of Midhurst (the great-grandfather) she preferred to forget. If Mary Susan had her eye on the main chance, life was presenting her with chances worth taking.

Why she was singled out by her so-called 'guardian' to be educated on a different level from her sisters is unclear, but the Victorians were mysterious people who often acted strangely. Augustus J. C. Hare wrote of the way he was adopted, and of how his mother, receiving a petition to let him go, replied at once: 'My dear Maria, how very kind of you! Yes, certainly, the baby shall be sent as soon as it is weaned; and if any one else would like one, would you kindly recollect that we have others.'

Possibly the guardian in Baker Street found Mary Susan more attractive than the other children, and decided to single her out for a ladylike education.

Miss Tempest had done a good deal of complicated knitting, if not embroidery, when talking to her biographer. She had described her grandmother as living in a house with a heavy oak door with a wide marble staircase, which she ascended wearing heavy, flounced silk or tussore dresses with lawn and linen petticoats. On Sunday the grandmother wore a mushroom bonnet with a veil of black and white chantilly lace, and a brooch of lapis lazuli with diamonds, and heavy earrings also of diamonds, while a gold pocket watch was enshrined in its own special pocket.

How odd it was that her grandmother did not seem to have a husband, she confided to her biographer. Had she any letters or papers about her grandmother? Nothing, nothing at all. Miss Tempest told Mr. Bolitho very definitely that she preferred to live in the present. She was, of course, much happier describing her 'guardian' who showed her his wonderful folding military furniture, his medals from the Crimea and the Indian Mutiny, and who grandly sent his servant to fetch her an ice-cream from a Baker Street *pâtisserie*. When she lifted the frilled paper from the ice-cream – there was a real strawberry. He had, of course, given her a wonderful doll's pram.

Having disposed of her childhood in a haze of romance, Miss Tempest began to draw a veil of chiffon over her early career which also bore all the hallmarks of a salad of fact and fiction.

While she was at the Royal Academy of Music she had met Julia Neilson who had decided to be an actress, and not a singer. Mary Susan was immediately taken with this good idea, and resolved to copy Julia's example. This horrified her respectable grandmother who resolved to bring some heavy guns to bear on her grand-daughter. According to Miss Tempest her grandmother went to see her friend Mrs. Gladstone at No. 10 Downing Street to try to persuade her away from this course.

In Miss Tempest's confidences to her biographer, she gave the impression that her grandmother (in her rustling silks) just called in casually to see Mrs. Gladstone in Downing Street. She mentioned her problems to the Prime Minister's wife, who sat in her armchair wearing a cap and mittens. On hearing about the projected stage career, she raised her mittened hands in protest saying: 'Oh, not the stage! Not the stage!'

'You see, Mrs. Gladstone, it's this Signor Garcia at the Academy. She has got on so well with her singing – she has met a girl called Julia Neilson there, who is going on the stage. I suppose I was wrong to allow her to learn singing at all. It's put the idea in her head.'

That sounds much more like the voice of the upper servant asking for advice, than a friend dropping in to see the Prime Minister's wife.

The story could have been partly true. It might have been that Mrs. Gladstone (on bowing terms with Mrs. Marriage, wife of the Yeoman at the Chapel Royal) had been written to in careful copperplate asking her to dissuade the child from this decadent step, and the subsequent interview was another example of that excellent condescension on the part of the upper classes trying to put the lower orders on the right path.

According to Miss Tempest, Mrs. Gladstone said: 'I must ask William to speak to the child.' She then trotted out to fetch him. Mary Susan and her grandmother waited for a long time, and eventually Mrs. Gladstone returned with the Prime Minister. Miss Tempest still remembered his impressive voice and manner, and how he had talked endlessly about the Greek Drama, of morality plays, of the coming of women on to the stage, and finally of the heinousness of the stage as a career for any young woman. If true, it was a curiously hypocritical performance. Gladstone and his wife were keen theatre-goers, and he, himself had even been seen (by mistake) on the stage in one of Irving's productions.

In 1884 when Marie Tempest, still Mary Susan Etherington, and still studying under Garcia at the Academy, was only twenty, her grandmother died. According to the official account, the old lady's dying words were: 'Mary, I am going to join my Maker. I shall not see you again. Dress well, my child, remember that – for you will never be anything without it.' No doubt, Mrs. Marriage found the wearing of one good silk dress stood her in good stead with the gentry.

Miss Tempest alleged that her grandmother, having died so inopportunely before she herself had been fairly launched in her career, had left all her money to the church. She had to sell the gloomy house in Whitehall and all the handsome furniture. The truth was perhaps, that both her grandparents had died, or maybe only her grandfather, and that the house and furniture were part of the job.

Mary was left without resources, but not without resource. The solution to her problems seemed, to her practical mind, to be a husband who would keep her while she advanced her career. She had a number of admirers at the Academy. It was an *embarras de choix*, and her eye fell on Alfred Izard. He was to be her solace and support. Her father had died in 1880. What had happened to the blond soldier who had paid for her education was not disclosed. Possibly he had also heard the blowing of the last bugle.

So in 1885 Mary Susan Etherington married Alfred Izard. He is dismissed very early in the story as a youthful mistake.

> My young husband wished me to be both Patti and Mrs. Beeton. He liked the glamour of my little success at the Academy, but this was not enough! Oh, no! He wished me to throw my career aside and mend his socks, and fuss about food when I came home.

This was not at all Miss Etherington's idea of bliss, and she walked out. Mr. Izard was obviously not going to be the provider and background which her budding talent needed. According to her account, she preferred to stand alone. Her subsequent career does not so much indicate standing alone as using others to forward her ambitions. But apart from the discipline of ambition, she had qualities which lifted her above the normal run of pretty girls who could sing. Because she was not pretty, she needed other attributes.

One of the best descriptions of her attractions was given by James Douglas in his *Adventures in London*.

> There are no dull moments in Marie Tempest, for she seems to have been made without melancholy. Her eyes are her life and soul. When you think of Marie Tempest you think of the incomparable eyes in which all the imps and humour and the gnomes of mischief are always dancing. She has the heart of a tomboy with the brain of a coquette. She is all impulse and impudence, lightness and levity, insouciance and elegance, frolic and fun. She can be gracefully gauche and wittily vulgar. She is a bundle of fascinating contradictions, and charming incongruities. She is an

artist to the tip of her adorable little tip-tilted nose which is always turning itself up at everything in this solemn old humbug of a world.

That was how her admirers and her audience saw her. That was the finished product. It had taken Miss Tempest a good many years of striving to create it. Officially there was a ten year gap between her first marriage to the music student Alfred Izard, and her second to the socially eligible Cosmo Gordon-Lennox (Cosmo Stuart the playwright), son of Lord Alexander Gordon-Lennox. But there was a missing piece in the story of Miss Tempest's lonely struggles. In 1888 she gave birth to a son who was called Normal Loring.

Norman was ten years old at the time of her second marriage in 1898, but as her marriage to Alfred Izard was dissolved a year after the birth, the child must presumably have had something to do with her husband being able to cut the shackles that bound him to her.

The birth of Norman coincided with her original successes in musical comedy, and on that account it might be considered relevant. She 'replaced' Marion Hood as the heroine of *Dorothy*, the musical play which made her a star, and it could have been that her sudden and startling success might have been due to a helping hand from an admiring manager. When recounting her early struggles Miss Tempest took great pride in the fact that, from the age of seventeen she kept herself. At twenty-five she was moderately rich, entirely due to her own efforts. But little Norman was born when she was twenty-four, was he the reason she had suddenly become so comfortably placed?

Miss Tempest waxed very indignant at the idea that actresses succeeded upon the patronage of lascivious managers. Ridiculous! They would not risk £20,000 to pander to their mistresses. No one had ever offered to make *her* a star on those conditions. Was the older Miss Tempest's indignation on the subject due to its truth?

By the time she started her musical comedy career Mary Susan Etherington had taken the name of Marie Tempest – Marie because that was the name she was given in Belgium, and Tempest after her supposed godmother Lady Susan Vane-Tempest.

Until her first big success in *Dorothy*, Miss Tempest readily admitted that she had been dogged by bad luck. Other actresses proved to be jealous of her. Kate Munro, the good hearted American actress, had taken her under her wing – and then behaved abominably to her. So abominably that the young Miss Tempest used to kneel down and pray (in the dressing-room) that God would kindly look down on her – and spare her an encore. Her prayers were answered. But God, as he so often does, chose a different way to answer her prayers. Poor Miss Munro faded from her star billing, and Marie Tempest took her place as 'queen of light opera'. *Dorothy* ran from 1886 to 1889. Miss Tempest took over from Marion Hood in 1887. But as Miss Tempest's only child was born on 8 May 1888, there must surely have been a sudden 'illness' for her temporary exit and his entrance.

From the beginning of her career, her relations with managements were stormy. She admitted it. 'I was more disliked than liked by managers, for I was a self-important little baggage, with a hot temper.' She rowed with Madame Melnotte, who was running the Comedy Theatre. Everyone called Violet Melnotte 'Madam', and Madam claimed that she had sacked Miss Tempest not once, but twice. But as Marie Tempest on both occasions managed to get herself a better job, no one believed Miss Melnotte.

On the second occasion, in 1890, she was engaged to appear in America with the J. C. Duff Light Opera Company. She sang in New York, and on tour, in various operas and comic operas, in roles varying from Mabel in *The Pirates of Penzance* to Carmen in Bizet's opera. She was professionally successful in America, but not liked by the press who considered her 'snooty'. She was already developing that grand manner which did not please the democratic Americans. Although her appearance, always her strong point, did. 'Little Marie Tempest trotted up Broadway, yesterday, looking very natty and refreshing. Miss Tempest dresses very quietly for the street. Other actresses might emulate her example.'

Success came to her easily on the New York stage as it had in London, and she spent five years in the United States either touring or acting on Broadway. If she did not entirely please off stage, on stage she was considered 'captivating' and presented for the Americans 'blue blood, aristocracy and that sort of thing'. It was said she had a curious trick of bending her arm when she shook hands as if saying 'keep off you must not trespass', but others said she extended her hand as if she expected it to be kissed in the continental manner rather than rudely shaken.

In American her voice pleased, although it was not to the taste of W. S. Gilbert who considered that she 'shrieked' on the top notes. But then it is impossible to please everybody, and Gilbert may not have been impressed by her kittenish manner, nor was he moved as one reporter had been by 'a lovely mouth and a pair of eyes that can smile with the archness of a coquette and almost at the same time reveal a world of passion'. Or possibly her tart manner and determination to get the better of managers had little appeal.

Reminiscing about life in New York Marie Tempest said, 'In the eighties people still entertained in their homes in London. I had seldom eaten in a restaurant. I revelled in the New York restaurants – Sherry's, Delmonico's, and Martin's.' A taste for restaurants was to remain with her.

On her return to London she went on singing in light opera, but it appeared that she was beginning to tire of the musical comedy stage. By one of those happy accidents which sometimes surprise leading ladies, she was lunching at the Savoy when she appears to have picked up Mr. Cosmo Gordon-Lennox – having been introduced to him by the gentleman's friendly dog. A few months after this canine introduction, she married Cosmo. At last the facts of her life were beginning to bear out the fiction she had invented. Cosmo was the grandson of the 5th Duke of Richmond and Gordon, his grandmother, the Lady Caroline Paget, daughter of the Marquess of Anglesey. Like Pope's heroine in the *Rape of the Lock* the soft sounds of 'your grace' were sounding in the shell-like ears of Miss Tempest, if at several removes. But this was more like it.

Long afterwards she freely admitted that she did incline to reflect the mind and tastes of the men who had been her producers, or her friends. 'I naturally borrow colour from other people', she said. Up to the moment of this fortuitous meeting with Cosmo she had, she felt, been a limited rather stupid little person with no knowledge of anything. She had sensed security and a chance to learn about the fashionable world she was to mirror so well on the stage. She moved into a splendid house, and, even better, she was no longer dependent on her own earnings, or the whims of managers. She had achieved at one stroke – a husband to keep her, a rich background, and eventually a resident playwright, who was to write *The Marriage of Kitty*, one of the most successful of the comedies in which she played.

The World described the Gordon-Lennoxes' house in Park Crescent as having extensive views over Regent's Park. Cosmo was descended from Charles II and Louise de Querouaille. His house was graced by her portrait by Sir Peter Lely and also boasted a Van Dyck of the Duke of York and his brothers, and a Romney of the 3rd Duke of Richmond. Miss Etherington had fallen plushly on her feet. Mrs. Gordon-Lennox (said *The World*) liked to relax in her chintzy boudoir chatting to her little green parrot who called her 'Marie'. She also rode in the Park on her horse 'Katy', accompanied by her sweet collie 'Ness', and her equally sweet little fox terrier 'Toby'.

What little Norman was doing during these displays of Belle Epoque magnificence was not revealed. He was presumably tucked away in some discreet prep school in the country. While her son was slogging through his conventional education, little Miss Tempest was equipping herself for her future role as Queen of Comedy. With the aid of Cosmo's bank balance and large outlook, Mrs. Cosmo Gordon-Lennox took a firm decision to leave the sordid purlieus of musical comedy. The year was 1900.

In a sudden burst of frankness she spoke of the past. 'You must remember that, in one way, I am rather like one of those glorified French cocottes. I absorb atmosphere and taste from others. A French cocotte can rise above her simple surroundings on the wings of her patron and learn manners, learn to absorb the culture of the man who influences her. She may learn to dominate his salon with wit and grace.'

Belle Epoque magnificence. Mr. Cosmo Gordon-Lennox and Miss Marie Tempest

As her friendly biographer Mr. Bolitho listened to the elegant Miss Tempest, in her charming house furnished with such exquisite taste, he could smile at the simile. What he did not realise was that Miss Tempest was telling him the simple truth.

'People', she went on, 'have always said that my method is French. Why? Because Cosmo was devoted to the Comédie Française school, and I listened to him and went to Paris so often during that impressionable time when I was learning to act.' Cosmo had taught her to think for herself, her life had opened out, and become larger in every way. She had also been taught exactly how to behave

69

in a grand social milieu but she did not mention that. The background of her imagination had become a reality. Her hands, beautiful but tiny, were said to be used with dominion and grace; they were now ready to pluck the fruits of success.

She found an author – Anthony Hope – a play, *English Nell*, and she was launched with quantities of expensive period clothes, designed by herself. Her studies with Cosmo, and Cosmo's splendid historical background, had enabled her to bring Nell Gwynn to life. Even *The Times* was delighted with her portrayal, and suggested that she should try even higher flights, for she had all the qualities of Lady Bancroft. *The Times* had little need to worry, little Mrs. Gordon-Lennox had a very wary eye on those higher flights.

In the process of achieving her success on the legitimate stage – she had been unlucky again. She had managed to annoy two leading actresses, Ellen Terry for whom *English Nell* had originally been written, and her dear friend from the old Academy of Music days, Julia Neilson, who 'by a strange coincidence' was just about to act in *Sweet Nell of old Drury*. Although there was nothing sweet in her thoughts about Miss Tempest.

From 1900 to 1908 Marie Tempest acted in a series of successes. With her newly acquired social flair she was able to portray the grand ladies who figured so largely in the plays of the period. In 1901 she played Becky Sharp with great success and éclat, although her detractors were of the opinion that in the part of Becky she was merely reflecting the methods of her own rise to fame and fortune.

Her marriage to Cosmo had given her a good deal. But chatting to her friendly biographer thirty years later, she was able to look back on this alleged early tragedy with tenderness. Alas, the years had brought sadness to Miss Tempest, but she was able to see the past without bitterness. It was a union doomed not to last.

In 1908, while she was playing in *Lady Barbarity*, a period piece about the French Revolution, she met William Graham-Browne. She fell in love with him, she admitted it simply: 'Seeing his blue eyes and his long lashes, I said to myself "That is the man who will make my life happy." ' Miss Tempest had found a fellow actor who attracted her. He was six years younger than she, and had all the qualities which she lacked.

In that same lucky year she found a play by that rising young playwright Mr. Somerset Maugham – *Mrs. Dot*, and followed it up in the following year by playing the leading role in *Penelope* by the same author. She was admirably suited to playing Mr. Maugham's charming, feline, scheming ladies, who twisted the gentlemen round their fingers, and always won in the end.

When the war broke out in 1914, poor Cosmo, like the gallant fellow he was, typical of his class and background, went to the Front to serve in the Medical Corps. More prudent than he, Miss Tempest sailed for America taking Mr. Graham-Browne with her. Those who had started at the top might be able to jeopardise their careers, those who had clawed their way up, could not afford to be so altruistic.

What was happening to Miss Tempest's son during the years of Miss Tempest's glory? He had been educated at Harrow and Trinity College, Cambridge. Did his father pay for his education, or did Miss Tempest? She was aware of the value of education and possibly she shouldered that burden. She could well have afforded to do so. From 1911 to 1913 Norman Loring served in the Indian Army. The Empire was a useful place for sending awkward people to, and in those days India was three or four weeks away on the other side of the world. In 1914 he came back to London where he appeared in two plays. He seems to have followed his mother to New York, for he appeared in her comedy, *Mary Goes First*. Why she gave him a part in one of her plays is not known, perhaps because she felt she could not afford to keep him. Possibly he did not even know that she was his mother, she may have classed herself as an aunt, or a godmother, as was the habit in those days. It was possible that he was not a success on the stage, because in 1915 Norman, like Cosmo, went to France and served in the British Army from 1915 to 1919, and after the war he was on the Canadian General Staff until 1922. Maybe he felt happier as a soldier than as an actor.

Miss Tempest and Mr. Graham-Browne spent a happy war acting in New York, then on to Australia. From there they toured the world – Africa, India, Japan and the Phillipines. But while she may have been touring the colonies and making long dusty railway journeys across continents, she did not intend to let her standards slip, nor those of her actors and actresses. She insisted on all members of her Company changing into full evening dress before going along to the restaurant car for dinner. Ladies who had married into the aristocracy were under the necessity of showing the natives how to behave. Finally they arrived in China where Miss Tempest began her fine collection of jade, and paintings on silk. In New Zealand her acting brought new revelations of finesse to her future biographer Hector Bolitho.

Why did she spend so many years touring the world? Possibly to avoid scandal. Women of her generation were only too anxious to preserve their public image. She had an unacknowledged illegitimate son, and a husband living. She was probably keeping out of the way both of the War, and of any possible threat of scandal to her career. Life had taught her not to take risks.

In 1921 Cosmo Gordon-Lennox conveniently died, and Miss Tempest was able to marry Mr. Graham-Browne without fuss and bother. She was the respectable widow of a duke's grandson. Although she had been the faithful companion and close friend of Mr. Graham-Browne for some years, they were able to return triumphantly to London, honourably married, and able to take up the threads of their careers at the centre of the empire they had been touring.

Miss Tempest was now poised to become a pillar of the stage establishment. She also had an eye to the up-and-coming, and was determined to live in the present. Her judgment was occasionally faulty, but she had a capacity for retrieving mistakes. She turned down the part of Judith Bliss in Coward's *Hay Fever*, but afterwards acted in it with brilliant success. The same turn-down was experienced by St. John Ervine, but his play *The First Mrs. Fraser* starring Miss Tempest had a long run. To see her disposing of the tarty second wife of her husband in this play, was a mirror of feminine wiles at their best. It was generally conceded that she was a dragon to act against, and yet her disciplined attitude towards her work, and the production gained her the admiration of authors and directors alike.

After he had produced her in *Hay Fever*, Noël Coward remembered: 'having for so many years been a star in every sense of the word, she wastes no time on personal inhibitions or inferiority complexes'. He admired the way she took off her coat, and got down to the job of the moment, and with far less chi-chi than any actress he had met. She was more than amenable to direction, in fact she begged for it, and if the director's suggestions were intelligently and carefully phrased, and she had faith in him, she accepted his views. These two people of such totally different generations were lavish in their praise of one another because they were both professionals to the last eyelash. That was literally true of Miss Tempest, who counted seven false eyelashes to each eye every evening.

Nor was it only her acting which Mr. Coward admired. He felt she had more allure and glamour – and charm – than many women he knew in their twenties and thirties. 'When she steps on to the stage, a certain magic occurs, and this magic is in itself unexplainable, and belongs only to the very great.' He added that what impressed him most of all was her unspoken, but very definite, demand for good behaviour.

After Coward had directed her in one of her most successful roles as Fanny Cavendish in *Theatre Royal* by George Kaufmann, she was interviewed about Coward's methods of directing. After so many years of being directed by her understanding husband had she felt herself 'opposed' to Mr. Coward? Miss Tempest answered stoutly: 'Opposed? Of *course* not. I am wax in his hands. When I go to a first rehearsal I may have ideas about the part I am to play, but I do not know what I shall do with it.'

Always exquisitely and expensively dressed Miss Tempest and her actor-director husband brought money into the box office with a series of comedies which, although they may not always have pleased the critics, gave her a faithful following amongst the play-goers of the period. To the suburbs she represented a life of fashion, to the fashionable she mirrored the more printable aspects of their mode of existence. She had perfect timing and dominated the stage, and the play, from the moment of her first entrance.

Miss Tempest and her husband lived in a grand house in Avenue Road, Regent's Park, attended by faithful servants and a good cook. The mistress of the house, with her French education, appreciated good cooking, and after the theatre she occasionally gave little supper parties in her exquisite Chinese dining-room. Mr. Bolitho was enraptured with its elegance. 'Its walls are covered with dull gold paper, stripped from the tea boxes which she bought in China. The gold is faded enough to be no more than a background for the tall cases of carved jade pieces, and on the mantelpiece, two flam-boyant green parrots. In the centre are two translucent green jade bowls. The chairs are painted Chinese Chippendale, and the side tables are simple unadorned Chinese.' Miss Tempest had learned a great deal from Cosmo.

George Bishop, the theatre critic, described Miss Tempest's supper parties in her exquisite dining-room as being as beautifully produced as the plays in which she appeared. The dialogue was crisp and witty, the food delicious, and the minor part of the maid hovering in the shadows of the candlelit room was played with discreet unobtrusiveness.

In 1935, Miss Tempest's friend Mr. James Agate of the *Sunday Times* discovered that she had been on the stage for nearly fifty years and he felt it high time that the matter should be celebrated. Mr. Agate had been a close (and useful) friend to Marie Tempest and her husband Willie for many years. Agate's diaries are full of references to them, and letters from both Mary (as he called her), and Willie. He often described her holding court at the Ivy restaurant 'dove-like in grey furs', or at the Savoy 'in black with a pink ostrich feather hat'. Or writing to him from the provinces '*quelle vie de dog*', adding that she could not begin to tell her dearest Jimmie of the *savagery* of these places.

Miss Tempest's taste in food was so exquisite that she put even the bohemian Mr. Agate in a tizzy when he asked her to lunch to discuss her matinée. He had sent out for foie gras, asparagus, and sherry from Fortnums, nothing but the best for her. After luncheon, he noted, 'Mary looked at my photos of Sarah and Réjane and she deplored the lesser fame of the comedienne "who is never remembered".' Agate added: 'I fancy she hankers after stage immortality and wants to go on in the world's mind, I admire her art intensely, and her pluck, vivacity and youth even more.'

Her fiftieth anniversary took place at Drury Lane in May of 1935. It was one of those heartwarming occasions which brought tears to every eye, and the King and Queen Mary to the Royal box.

For this great day in her life, Marie Tempest chose to play the second act of *The Marriage of Kitty* in which she sang her little French song at the piano. Graham-Browne directed her, and played the solicitor in his usual unassuming way. Margaret Rawlings was the Peruvian widow, and Yvonne Arnaud, the French maid. The leading lady remembered every move of the original production, and as she said, did not vary her performance in movement, inflexion, or timing. Everything came back to her like a scene from her childhood. The only thing she had carefully chosen to forget was her second husband who had adapted the piece from the French. He had been long dead. She then played the cynical old Empress in *Little Catherine* and after giving her last authoritative command, tottered off to die. This was the tragic actress she had chosen never to be.

The souvenir programme was decorated with designs by Doris Zinkeisen and George Sheringham. The picture *Souvenir de Marie* by William Nicholson was reproduced. It shows a couch piled high with sequin trimmed taffeta skirts, fur-edged satin petticoats, silk stockings, long white gloves, and a black hat trimmed with ruched ribbons and an ostrich feather, and on a velvet stool a pair of pink satin mules. In the oval mirror reflected like a distant small shade the actress is coming into her elegant dressing-room. Miss Tempest was noted for her love of adornment, she had remembered the advice of her grandmother: 'Dress well my child, you will never be anything without it.'

Eminent musicians – Sir Edward German and Sir Landon Ronald – lauded her. The writers of the day praised her with discerning words. St. John Ervine wrote: 'She has shed the lustre of her intelligent laughter on our stage for half a century. In all her acting has been the thoughtful laughter which Meredith insisted is the spirit of comedy.'

Noël Coward remembered the first time he had seen her in 1912.

74

She was playing at the Prince of Wales Theatre in a comedy called *At the Barn*. I remember a short blue and mauve taffeta dress with panniers, and one of her usual crisp little hats. I also remember two minutes of silent acting at the end of the first act which, even at the tender age of 12, I was bright enough to brand into my memory, where it has remained clear and unexcelled by anything I have since seen in the theatre. Marie Tempest sat alone with a handkerchief in her right hand, and a sandwich in her left, deciding in her troubled mind whether to eat, or to weep. Finally, the tears won, and the sandwich went back on to the plate, and the handkerchief to her eyes.

Somerset Maugham wrote sensibly of her patience, punctuality, and precision, underlining the qualities which appealed to him.

Others will have written of Marie Tempest's wonderful talent, of her charm, and irresistible gaiety; it may have escaped the notice of many who have admired her brilliant performances that they are due not only to her natural gifts, which are eminent, but to patience, assiduity, industry and discipline. Without these it is impossible to excel in any of the arts. But that is something that not all who pursue them know.

There was no well known actor or actress who did not participate in the tribute to Miss Tempest's fame, some even in the humble capacity of programme sellers. Even the ticket agencies refused their commission for the grand occasion.

The afternoon ended with a players' Masque in which John Gielgud (playing Mercury), led the shadows of the players of the past, and of the present, before the Cerberus of a stage door keeper until the huge stage was filled with actors doing homage to the great comedienne who was carried high above them in a golden chair.

The applause and excitement rained down on her. She confessed that she was overwhelmed, and sinking into her always graceful curtsy remained the devoted and humble servant of her public, as she had been these fifty years. A dedicated, disciplined player who had battled her way upwards from humble origins to scribble her bold signature on a vellum scroll on which hundreds of her fellow players had signed their names, and now hers was to be added to the signatures of the King and Queen. It had been a long and arduous journey, and she had accomplished it with will power, and without good looks.

Two years later Graham-Browne died. It was one of the greatest shocks of her life. Her husband was six years her junior and it was a most unexpected blow. Yet she still soldiered on.

In 1938 she played in her last success, *Dear Octopus* by Dodie Smith. She played the grandmother Dora Randolph, surrounded by her children, grandchildren, and her loving, large, if sometimes tiresome family. No one who saw her will forget the break in her voice as she sang: 'Oh, the days of the Kerry dancing! Oh the ring of the pipers' tune! Oh for one of those hours of gladness, gone alas like our youth too soon.' Perhaps she was remembering the desperate ambitious youth of her own which had gone too soon. Her hands had been filled with worldly gifts, but the family around her were only a stage family engaged for the run of the piece. Her husband, her support and joy had gone. Her son was a hidden quantity. She was alone with her fame. Yet she moved about the stage as exquisitely dressed as ever in soft black taffeta, or in gold lamé for her fiftieth wedding anniversary in the play, a fiftieth anniversary she had never shared with dear Willie.

The 1939 War broke out, and Miss Tempest went back to her *vie de dog* of touring. In the spring of 1942, James Agate wrote that she was up and about again after her illness, and 'holding court at the Ivy'.

Some time later that year Henry Kendall was asked to produce a play called *The Grand Manner*. He took the job because he wanted to work with Marie Tempest. The first rehearsal was to be held in the Dome at the top of His Majesty's Theatre. When he got there (five minutes early), he found the Dame sitting in a high-backed chair glowering. She was wearing scarlet slacks, a green jumper, and a saucy hat with a pheasant's feather stuck in the side. As the rest of the cast drifted in, Miss Tempest addressed them: 'Why are you late? If an old woman like me can be punctual, why can't you? Can't bear unpunctuality.' The first reading of the play went on, and eventually lunch was mentioned. 'Lunch!' barked Dame Marie, 'Lunch! Who wants lunch? I never lunch when I'm rehearsing. We will go on until three o'clock, then I shall go home to bed until seven, and we will work this evening until ten!'

The rehearsals proceeded on their way. She was easy to produce and everyone settled down. The actors gradually relinquished their 'books' and became word perfect. All except Miss Tempest, the star, who did not know one line. The truth dawned. Her memory had gone. The management decided that Miss Tempest must go. Henry Kendall was appalled. He looked at her. She was seventy-eight, surely he could give her one more chance? But it was useless. The words had gone for ever. So many plays, so many songs, so many rehearsals, for nearly sixty years.

Marie Tempest with dear Willie

Henry Kendall (reinforced by William Mollison) took the old lady into the Royal Box. She sat stiffly in the King's armchair. She heard the verdict. For a long moment she said nothing. Then in the half-darkness of the box, they saw two tears trickling down her face. In her husky voice, she whispered without complaint: 'I quite understand – will someone please fetch me a taxi?'

Henry Kendall wrote: 'I escorted her to the stage door, and into the waiting taxi. "Good-bye, dear Mary." ' It was the first time he had dared to call her that. 'And thank you!' He stood there for a long moment watching the taxi carrying her away from her last rehearsal.

She had once said: 'I have only two interests in the world, one is my home life with my husband, and the other is my work.'

Willie, her husband and companion, was dead. His death had been a disaster for her, compounded by the outbreak of war. The exquisite background of furs and frocks in which she had moved had disappeared. It was no longer possible to stroll down Piccadilly on a sunny morning wearing a crisp little hat.

She had much in common with Mr. Maugham in whose early pieces she had shone. She had given everything to her public face, and to her small exquisite art of comedy. Like Becky Sharp, Miss Tempest had come a long way, and had achieved much. It was now time to shut up the box, and put the puppets away. The performance was over.

THE SEVEN YEAR HITCH
or
Lord Francis Shoots Wide

In January of 1893 Miss May Yohé was interviewed by a reporter who called himself 'Call Boy'. She was among thirty-five currently successful actresses whom Call Boy had chosen to feature in his forthcoming book *On and Off* – one of those effusions which paint untruthful glimpses of actresses away from the footlights, but which give the public the illusion that they are being let into the inner secrets of beauty, romance, and success.

Miss Yohé was to give only brief glimpses of her background to her London interviewer. Her father was an ironfounder from Pennsylvania, and she was supposed to have been educated in convents in France and Germany, where she had shocked the nuns by announcing that she had decided not to become a 'postulant' – an apprentice nun – but to be an actress and a singer. Whether the shock of the nuns was due to the poor quality of her voice, or her choice of profession was not revealed.

Her stage career began at a Chicago theatre when she was eighteen. An English actress, who was in the same company, said May Yohé was a pretty piquant brunette with a contralto voice. Her eyes were set on London, then the rich luxurious centre of an Empire. She rejected offers from American companies – Europe was calling. Possibly piquant brunettes were more unusual the other side of the Atlantic. American critics admitted her attractions, but noted her faults. 'Miss Yohé had attained fame in spite of severe handicaps. Most critics were agreed that she had a poor stage presence and no marked ability; that her attractions were limited to a clear complexion, a pair of flashing electric black eyes, and a vibrant throaty voice.' Another American added: 'She has only four notes in her voice, but they are corkers!' She had not had much success in America, in spite of her vibrant voice, and flashing eyes. But once she came to London she had all the advantages of looking, and sounding, exotic.

How she managed the leap from touring in America to leading parts on the West End stage is difficult to discover. Some accounts say that she was introduced to London managers by Lord Francis Pelham-Clinton-Hope, brother of the Duke of Newcastle. Other reports merely announce baldly that she 'came to London in 1893'.

Her first appearance on the London stage was the reason for Call Boy's interview. 'The lady I have worried the most in connexion with this book of interviews, and to whom in consequence I owe the greatest number of apologies, is Miss Yohé.' Call Boy went on to describe the attractions which had led him to her dressing-room:

The olive-complexioned, hazel eyed, neat figured beauty who in the character of a gipsy stole away my heart on the first night of *The Magic Opal*, on Thursday 19 January 1893 at which time Miss May Yohé made her bow to the admiring British public.

And, some reports say, to the admiring Lord Francis Pelham-Clinton-Hope in his private box.

In *The Magic Opal*, dressed in her gipsy costume, she had made an instant hit with a song 'Many and many a weary mile'. With her invigorating transatlantic zest, it was simple to see why Miss Yohé, with her non-existent voice had amazed the British public. They were used to simpering girls with frills purveying sweetness, Miss Yohé was giving them a touch of tabasco.

After apologising for troubling her, and being told that she did not mind – always provided that Mr. Call Boy interviewed her at express speed, she couldn't keep the stage waiting for *him* – Mr. Call Boy plunged straight into the question which had been puzzling him.

'Who was the trainer of your extraordinary voice?'

'The owner, Mr. Call Boy.'

'You surprise me.'

'I've surprised a good many.'

And as things were to turn out, she was to surprise a good many more.

'It's a fact', went on Miss May. 'I trained it to run on its course – and a very limited one it is too.'

Miss Yohé was pulling no punches, she was proud of her success. She had had at one time she admitted, a soprano voice, but on her way home from finishing school at Dresden – it had broken – just like –

Mr. Call Boy interrupted her with a heavy joke which had occurred to him, 'A bit of Dresden china?'

'No! Like a boy's voice.'

Nothing deterred, Mr. Call Boy plugged on with his joke. 'I see, unlike a bit of china it broke before it dropped!'

It is possible to imagine the look the pedestrian Mr. Call Boy received from the flashing black eyes of Miss Yohé. He decided on a spoonful of flattery.

'Do you know, Miss Yohé, that yours is the sort of voice that goes right to the heart?'

'Is it? Well, perhaps that is because it comes straight from it – at least from the chest – which is somewhere in the neighbourhood.'

Miss Yohé was a down-to-earth girl who was not to be overcome by compliments from cooing reporters.

'You made your first appearance on the stage in your own country – did you not?'

'Yes, in farcical comedy.' She outlined a number of plays in which she had appeared which from their titles hardly fell into the category of intellectual entertainment, concluding with a version of the *Arabian Nights* in which she played an exotic Eastern Princess.

'In all of which you were a big success?'

'You can put that down – if you like,' said Miss Yohé truthfully, 'I'm sure it can't do any harm. I don't think it is altogether untrue. After my Chicago engagement, I toured Australia – having a good time on the way.'

Was it while 'having a good time' that she perhaps met Lord Francis?

'I went back to America – and then played in the successful *Hoss and Hoss*.'

'In which, I hope you saw a good deal of the oof.'

Mr. Call Boy was allowing himself another heavy joke; 'oof' was Victorian slang for money.

'I don't know about *that*,' said Miss Yohé, 'but we used to see a good deal of the oof of the cowboys when we were playing to them in a wild neighbourhood in Montana. When they're satisfied with the show there – they pelt you with money.'

'How beastly, and what do they do when they're not satisfied?'

'Can't say, but I can tell you this – that time's up – and you must bid me good-bye and get!'

Mr. Call Boy wrote that he bade her good-bye and got!

Her next success after her appearance as the Gipsy in *The Magic Opal* was in *Mam'zelle Nitouche*, which was put on at the Trafalgar Theatre by Miss Violet Melnotte. The play called on Miss Yohé to act the part of a convent girl – Denise de Flavigny, and the lady from Pennsylvania was photographed in this piece, looking suitably demure, with her black hair hanging down her back, gazing soulfully at a lily in a pot. The settings included the convent (complete with resident Mother Superior), the Green Room at the Pontracy Theatre and, for some reason, a barrack yard. A contemporary, who had seen her as Mam'zelle Nitouche, was as overcome as her interviewer, Mr. Call Boy. 'Her singing, though faulty in method, had a quality which made it quite distinctive. Her voice was amazing: a contralto with deep chest notes which echo unforgettably in the memory. The very first notes of it that fell on the ear, when she made her first entrance in *Mam'zelle Nitouche* as one of those three veiled demure convent girls, evoked admiring, wondering attention, as do the deep notes of a silver cornet. The voice alone would have won her success in that character – independent of the vivacity and impulsive humour with which the actress played it.'

Mr. William Archer, the eminent critic, remained unmoved by Miss Yohé's deep chest notes, flashing eyes, and long black hair. 'The comic opera has degenerated into a rough-and-tumble absurdity, with musical interludes of a music hall type in which Miss Yohé abandoned herself to a series of gambols which highly amused the audience.'

But patently not Mr. Archer.

Her next success was *Little Christopher Columbus*. This time one of the leading light music composers of the day had been engaged to write her songs. Although the American critics said she had only four notes to her voice, the English critics gave her five or six, but what she had she was determined to exploit to the full. Ivan Caryll, operating within the limits of Miss Yohé's voice, had written her the earliest of the coon songs, 'Honey, oh ma honey', the song which was to give her instant fame on the London stage.

Just before the opening of the piece, when she was interviewed, she admitted that the music of *Little Christopher Columbus* had to be specially written for her by Ivan Caryll 'crammed so to speak within my voice's shrunken circumference'. Truthful, and without pretence, Miss Yohé made no apologies for her voice. The public had accepted it, and so did she.

Interviewed about the same time by a lady reporter on *The Sketch*, avid for sartorial details for her lady readers, Miss Yohé showed the more feminine side of her nature.

'The charming piquant figure of Miss May Yohé handsomely gowned in a harmony of autumnal tints, well-suited to her clear olive complexion, dark, wavy hair, and brilliant hazel eyes arose from a settee in her drawing-room to greet me.'

The lady reporter was astonished at the idea that Miss Yohé was to play a boy's part, but she supposed that Little Christopher Columbus must be a male descendant of the discoverer of the New World.

'It's yes – and no – to your question. I am going to play a boy's part, and a girl's part as I shall endeavour to represent all the gaucherie of a boy who is masquerading in girl's clothes.'

The lady reporter then plunged into the subject which really interested her – and her readers.

'If rumour speaks true you are to have some lovely dresses?'

'My word – you're right! There is a pink one just right up-to-date, I can tell you, the cutest thing you ever saw with three flounces. And another made out of 100 yards of silk with five different shades of yellow. And a Spanish one with a *divine* hat. I am going to show you all the new way to wear a veil. . . . While as to gloves, stockings, and my parasol – well, they're coming straight from Paris, France.'

'Didn't you go to Paris to study the Goulue dance?'

'Oh yes. But an *English* public would never stand it as it is danced there, and I have to tone it down. I shall give a sort of can-can, then a minuet, and a negro dance with a plantation ditty – but I shan't black up.'

Miss Yohé was not entirely on the side of the British audience, in spite of her success. When she was asked whether she preferred English or American audiences, she was quite frank.

'Why American to be sure! I have nothing to say against your upper circle, gallery or pit, but my word! The stalls! Why they just sit with their eyes under the seats.'

Then carried away by the idea of America she remembered her cowboys.

'For a real good time give me a cowboy audience. Well there! That's something like! In a wild part of Montana, it was in a barn like place, the dressing-rooms were only recesses fixed up on either side of the stage, with just a couple of "crazy" quilts to screen them. There was only one cake of soap, and one pot of rouge among us. We had to throw them across the stage to one another, and we had only the light of candles to dress by. But what a night it was, and what a house it was!'

The lady reporter from *The Sketch* remarked primly that Miss Yohé seemed to have a great deal of sympathy with the Wild West.

'I should think I have! Though my father's family hails from Holland, I can trace clear descent from the brave Nagarasette tribe of Indians. Yes, sir, I am a real American, and as proud as Lucifer that I can say so!'

The lady reporter, taken aback by this frank admission of Yankee superiority, changed the subject. Had she not heard something about Miss Yohé's lucky dress? On this question Miss Yohé was able to gush happily to the satisfaction of the lady from *The Sketch*.

'You are alluding to my *Mascotte* dress, which my dear mother

83

made for me, and which I wore in *The Magic Opal* and *Mam'zelle Nitouche* because it has always brought me luck.' Miss May Yohé was prepared to admit to some feminine weaknesses.

'I am awfully superstitious. Do you know I really believe in black cats?'

She then went on to recount that directly one of her plays came to an end her black cat died, or mysteriously disappeared. But – before the beginning of a new show *another* black cat was always given to her. In the case of a series of flops, Miss Yohé's superstition would seem to demand a constant and fresh supply of black cats, but this was not remarked on by the lady reporter, dazzled by Miss Yohé, her setting, her appearance, her clothes, and above all by her success.

Little Christopher Columbus fared no better than her other efforts with the critics, in spite of the music by Ivan Caryll and the 'book' by George R. Sims and Cecil Raleigh. *The Times* remarked that this piece seemed to mark the lowest attainable level of theatrical enterprise. The 'hit song' of the show featured Miss Yohé singing her coon song 'Honey, oh ma honey' wearing a plantation dress of big straw hat, white blouse, and striped knickers, with one leg turned up above the knee to add piquancy. But *The Times* was not to be influenced by rolled-up knicker legs, or coon songs, which possibly accounted for Miss Yohé's uncomplimentary views of the ladies and gentlemen in the stalls. Cowboys appreciated a little spunk, and showed that they did with showers of silver dollars.

But it was quite different with the public who took Miss Yohé to their heart. The Prince of Wales saw the piece twice, and the libraries reported such very good business that it ran for nearly a year.

Although some theatre historians report that Miss Yohé's success was due to an introduction from Lord Francis Pelham-Clinton-Hope, others allege that he was in the first night audience of *Little Christoper Columbus*. He had supposedly fallen under the spell of her four-note voice and had also been drawn to her neat figure, and rolled up knicker leg. It was unreliably reported that 'an introduction to her was effected by a mutual friend, and that their acquaintance rapidly ripened into something more than friendship'.

Lord Francis Pelham-Clinton-Hope's ancestry was impeccable, stretching back to Geoffrey de Clinton in the reign of Henry I, and included a Lord High Admiral. Lord Francis' brother was owner of the great Clumber House in Nottinghamshire.

A Victorian traveller's account waxed lyrical about Clumber, 'princely seat of the Duke of Newcastle. The principal rooms in this great house are the state dining-room, sixty feet long, thirty-four

Clumber House, princely seat of the Duke of Newcastle

feet wide, and thirty feet high; it can accommodate one hundred and fifty guests at dinner, with room to spare. The entrance hall is very lofty, and the roof supported by columns. The library of books is stated to be a most valuable collection.

'The park is about thirteen miles in circumference. But to my view the great ornament of Clumber, as of every other country house where there is such, is the fine sheet of water in front of it, on which there is, at least there was when I visited it many years ago, a good sized frigate, fitted and rigged in the most perfect manner, not a rope or block wanting, or out of place, the handiwork of some old sailor, who had left the perils of the sea to wield his crutch on land, and tell how battles had been fought and won.

'The state drawing-room is forty-eight feet long by thirty feet wide. The Library is of similar dimensions, and last but not least, so is the kitchen. There is also a private chapel, four of the windows in which cost £800 each. Here, as may well be supposed, are pictures and paintings "rich and rare". One room contains seven valued at £25,000.'

For a cotton-picking coon singer there was much to be picked up, and always the outside chance that – should something unfortunately happen to the Duke – Miss Yohé's admirer would inherit all this magnificence and she might stand a chance of becoming a duchess. There was much to reflect on for Miss Yohé, as she sang her coon song each evening.

In the autumn Miss Yohé was appearing in a piece by George Dance called *The Lady Slavey*. In the programme the music was noted as being composed by 'John Crook etc.' There was no mention of who 'etc' was. The plot was the well-worn one of Cinderella up-dated, but with a great stroke of originality the two ugly sisters had become two pretty sisters. They were setting their caps at the wealth and affections of an American millionaire called The Tomato King. Miss Yohé (playing the Cinderella role) was disguised as a parlourmaid, in order to back up the social pretensions of her two sisters. The chorus, as listed, appears to be a cross section of trades and occupations, consisting of butchers, bakers, milkmen, tradesmen, shop girls, milliners, dress-makers, and nursemaids. In the midst of this farrago the sparkling Miss Yohé pranced and sang.

'Who could look prettier than Miss Yohé,' wrote one critic, 'when dressed in the daintiest waiting maid's gown that a first-class milliner can design? Some critics may find fault with her singing, and her acting, but no observer can dispute her popularity.'

The picture of Miss Yohé as a parlourmaid swishing pertly about in her crisp print frock, with her equally crisp cap and apron bears out this view.

'Who could look prettier than Miss Yohé when dressed in the daintiest waiting maid's gown?'

During the run of this piece, Lord Francis Pelham-Clinton-Hope and the 'Lady Slavey' got married at the Hampstead Registry Office on 27 November 1894. The marriage was kept secret. Lord Francis was said to be as entirely independent as a man can be, and 'had better reason than most for assuming that his marriage was exclusively his own affair'. Another reason was possibly because Lord Francis' relatives would not have been overjoyed to know that he was bringing Red Indian blood into the family. He was not anxious to have troops of relations on the warpath, and perhaps feared his wife's straight from the shoulder remarks which might counter any disapproval.

Lord Francis was twenty-seven at the time he married, and was described 'as having many personal friends, although he was little known to the rest of the world. Occasionally misunderstood he was often said to be misrepresented, a fact to which he remained serenely indifferent.' The Press were understandably annoyed at not being let into the secret of the marriage, news of which did not come out for two or three months. Lord Francis took his bride to live at Deepdene near Dorking, a house which he had inherited from his mother.

Unlike many of her contemporaries on the stage, Miss Yohé, now the Lady Francis Pelham-Clinton-Hope, took no time off from *The Lady Slavey*, not even for a honeymoon. As she had explained to a reporter, her voice was considered unique and that very fact 'was detrimental to it in a way, because it would be *so* difficult to find an understudy'. Miss Yohé was not giving up any of the fame she had won to anyone. Perhaps she merely regarded her marriage as a long-term insurance policy. Sitting amidst the grandeur of Deepdene, or looking out on to the rhododendron bordered drive was hardly her idea of an amusing life, so she went on acting.

In 1896 she appeared in *The Belle of Cairo* by Cecil Raleigh and Kinsey Peile at the Royal Court Theatre. This appears to have been a mildly patriotic piece in which Lady Francis appeared as Pephtys, daughter of a carpet merchant. For some reason, possibly connected with the plot, she appeared in the second act disguised as a trumpeter singing about 'The Boys from Gordon's Home'.

> Far, far away from dear old England
> Beneath a Southern Sky
> He fought until the bitter ending
> And taught us how to die.
> He shed his life blood gladly
> For England and her fame.
> The wide world now reveres his memory
> And honours Gordon's name.

No doubt Miss Yohé's four husky notes added pathos to the song.

The customers at the Royal Court Theatre (boxes three guineas to £1.10s.6d, stalls half-a-guinea, and 7s.6d for the dress circle, and gallery 1s.) were pleased to applaud Lady Francis in her various disguises whether in the black robes of the carpet seller's daughter, or in her fetching drummer boy's outfit.

The lady reporter on *The Sketch* was given nearly two columns to describe the dresses, which were an essential part of the attraction of the piece. She gave her admiration full rein in describing frocks, galons, zouaves, pleats, roses, osprey feathers, bows and ruchings in such a way as to make the head of any male critic reel, especially if he happened to have less space than the lady reporter for his review of the actual play. But what a feast for feminine eyes, wrote the lady reporter, adding ecstatically 'And yet there are more new plays to come, and they nearly all promise us a *further* series of animated fashion plates for admiration and imitation.'

One male critic was not enchanted. '*The Belle of Cairo* shows some prettiness, and a few pleasant notes of oriental charm, but in the main the play relies on the sort of humour fully exploited by other members of this hybrid form of entertainment that has killed the comic opera, and almost scotched the drama.'

The characters in the play reflected the contemporary taste for exotic travel. The cast list included English aristocrats (assorted) on a tour, accompanied by l'homme from Cook's to protect them from Arabs, camels, deserts and Oriental mayhem. There were also contingents of the British Army, but why the forces needed Miss Yohé dressed as a drummer boy was not explained in the programme notes.

Miss May Yohé seems to have been quite happily married to Lord Francis for seven years. They had no children, and she continued to sing and dance on the West End stage. His hobby was an intense passion for shooting assorted game, but there is no indication that his wife, in spite of her Red Indian blood, shared his passion. Possibly her Red Indian streak told her that game was for eating, not for merely writing down in the game book of a stately home. All went well – Lady Francis shared all the comforts of Deepdene and the social round, while continuing to delight her audiences with her deep chest notes.

In 1900 – perhaps inspired by *The Belle of Cairo* – Lord and Lady Francis decided on a world cruise. Touching at various indicated points of interest they arrived in America. While they were there they met Putnam Bradlee Strong who was, as an English reporter remarked sarcastically, 'like so many Americans, a colonel'. Strong was a colonel in the New York state militia, and lived in New York City. By a curious coincidence in November of the same year, 1900, Miss Yohé was offered a part in a play opening on Broadway, and they went back to America and took an apartment at 215 West 34th Street.

Lord Francis settled his wife in the apartment, and a few weeks later left for Florida on a shooting expedition with the Duke of Newcastle, or as Miss Yohé might have put it, they were on a 'hunting' trip. It was not specified what kind of game Lord Francis and his brother were after. But it was quite certain the kind of game 'Colonel' Putman Bradlee Strong was after – it was Miss May, the Lady Francis. Lord Francis had asked May's aunt to come and act as chaperone to his wife while she was acting in New York. Whether the aunt never turned up, or whether she was told to make herself scarce by Putman Bradlee Strong was not clear.

Lord Francis, fresh from the great out-of-doors in Florida, made a brief visit to his wife in New York where during a little local socialising he met Putman. He then set sail for London where he had some family business to transact. Miss May was left in New York acting, and, as it turned out, being 'squired' by the redoubtable Putman.

At the end of March 1901, Lord Francis, having completed his business affairs, and presumably having seen the end of the shooting season, decided to rejoin his wife in New York. He had lived, at least to his own satisfaction, in amity and happiness with his wife for nearly seven years, and was shocked when he expected to be welcomed back into her loving arms, to be told that either he or she would have to leave the apartment. She bundled him into a cab and took him round to her solicitors where she announced, in front of witnesses, that she had absolutely decided not to live with him as his wife any longer.

Lord Francis, not a stayer, took this decision as final and sailed back to England. He could not understand the sea change in the sparkling Miss May. He was puzzled by his wife's attitude. What could have come over her? He tried to make some sense of her reiterated statements that she was determined 'to go her own way'. Prompted by his solicitors he decided to find out which way she was going.

He engaged some private enquiry agents, and soon discovered that when in New York, in his absence, his wife had not been chaperoned by her aunt, and what was more Colonel Putnam Bradlee Strong had been in the habit of dropping into the apartment, and staying the night there, as and when it suited him – and Lady Francis.

Sir Arthur Pinero wrote a play about a childless couple called *Mid Channel*, an Edwardian version of *The Seven Year Itch*, in which Miss Irene Vanbrugh suffered a great deal in richly trimmed gowns over the barrenness of her union. There was no such parallel for Lady Francis. Having announced that her marriage was over, she went her own way, and immediately left for San Francisco, accompanied by the Colonel.

In San Francisco the guilty couple were tracked down by the local newspapermen. They had registered as 'Mr. and Mrs. Hastings of Boston.' They were confronted by one reporter, who, filled with assumed Puritan virtue, challenged the supposed Mr. and Mrs. Hastings. 'We shall publish the truth! It is that you and your companion are entered in the hotel books under an assumed name!'

The Colonel spluttered. 'This is an outrage!'

The errant Lady Francis, spunky as always, was not in the least put out. All right, she was not married, so what? She decided on a simple explanation: 'It was because I got tired of Hope, that I became Strong.'

Totally undaunted, she left San Francisco, nipping off smartly in the S.S. *Nippon* bound for Japan, and registered herself and Putnam in the ship's passenger list unimaginatively as Mr. and Mrs. Smith.

By this time, Lord Francis decided he had been publicly humiliated enough. He had all the evidence he needed for a divorce and set the proceedings *en train*. During the family fracas when the news of the divorce had already been published, the Duke of Newcastle happened to visit San Francisco, and here, he in his turn was confronted by the same reporters who had tracked down his sister-in-law. He was chatty and affable with them, and quite ready to discuss his family affairs. 'While I am opposed on principle to divorce,' said the Duke blandly, 'I am not interfering.'

The reporters asked about the Hope diamonds.

'My sister-in-law did not have any of the Hope diamonds. What gems she did have is not my business,' he added loftily. What were a few diamonds here or there, when it was a question of getting rid of a woman who had been nothing but a headache to the family? That was what came of marrying people with Red Indian blood.

The case came up on 21 March 1902 before Sir Francis Jeune as Hope v. Hope and Strong.

Mr. Barnard (appearing for Lord Francis) asked a privilege of the court:

'May the petitioner be allowed to give his evidence seated in the well of the Court as he has recently met with a gun accident which necessitated the amputation of his foot?'

The President was sympathetic to this sporting injury, and immediately gave his permission for the petitioner to remain seated while he gave his evidence. The permission having been granted, the petitioner limped into the court, sat down and gave evidence in support of his divorce petition. When he accompanied the respondent to her solicitors in New York, she told him that if he did not go, she would clear out and leave him. That sentence has the right stalwart ring of 'Miss May', the darling of the cowboys. He begged her not to do so, but she insisted, and he returned to England the next day. When he heard of his wife's conduct with the respondent, he instituted the present suit.

The President: 'Was that the first you had heard of of her misconduct?'

The Petitioner: 'Yes.'

The President: 'You heard of no misconduct with Strong before?'

The Petitioner: 'No.'

Mr. Barnard (for Lord Francis) then read the affidavits of John and Louisa Blanche who were in the service of the respondent as butler and maid, leave having been given by the court to prove adultery by affidavit. The butler and maid were quite firm in their statements. The co-respondent had frequently slept in the apartment, and even occupied the same room as Lady Francis. They were not disposed to condone immorality, especially not in a former employer.

Not only that, they added in their statements that the Colonel and the lady had toured the country together visiting Baltimore, Washington, Boston, and Chicago, using different names in different cities. Presumably John and Louisa had been taken into the confidence of the lady and the Colonel and asked to forward letters. The old adage says place not your trust in princes; confidence in butlers and maids can be just as misplaced.

The final stage of the cross-continental journey of Lady Francis and her paramour ended at San Francisco. Finally, as had been stated said Lord Francis' counsel, they had sailed for Japan.

It was one time when Lieutenant Pinkerton was left behind, and Madam Butterfly had sailed in the opposite direction.

The President accepted the evidence of the butler and maid, and continued with the only witness present – the cuckolded Lord Francis.

The President: 'When you returned to America did you see Strong?'

The Petitioner: 'Yes, I saw him – but not often.'

The President: 'Did you know that he was constantly visiting Lady Francis?'

The Petitioner: 'I did not think he called more constantly than other people.'

The President was unused to dealing with such an unperceptive witness. Lord Francis may have had a keen eye for a bird on the wing, but he seemed singularly short-sighted when it came to a lover in his wife's bed.

The President: 'You entertained no suspicions?'

The Petitioner: 'No.'

The President could hardly credit such gullibility.

Lord Francis Pelham-Clinton-Hope. He had no suspicions whatever as to her conduct

The President: 'Did Lady Francis give you no reasons for desiring a separation?'

The Petitioner: 'No. She declined to give me any — although I repeatedly pressed her to do so.'

The Judge thought for a moment. It did not seem to him that any husband should be quite so stupid, so he decided to make a comment on the situation.

The President: 'I wish to make this quite clear, because it strikes me that your leaving your wife alone in New York in the way in

93

which you did was exposing her to temptation in a way which might be deprecated.'

Possibly the Judge felt that men who went off shooting leaving their pretty wives to the attentions of colonels in the New York militia had only themselves to blame if they lost their wives, or their feet.

The President: 'You tell me you had *no* suspicions whatever as to her conduct?'

The Petitioner: 'No.'

The Judge then seemed to lose interest in the case, and had no further remarks to make.

Lady Francis did not choose to make an appearance in court, or defend herself in any way. She had more interesting things to do with her life.

The President: 'Very well. There will be a decree nisi – with costs.'

Lord Francis married again, a lady from Melbourne, but the gallant Colonel did not manage to corral Miss May. She left him, and finally married Captain Smuts, nephew of the South African General Smuts, and disappeared from the history of the stage.

She was a lively lady with free and easy ideas, but possibly more impressed by cowboys than coronets.

A SPORTING EARL AND HIS HEIR VS.
THE ORGAN-GRINDER

On 2 September 1908, Sylvia Storey, lately of the chorus of a West End musical comedy became 7th Countess Poulett. But in the 1840s this seemed unlikely. Four lives were between William Henry Poulett, the son of Vice-Admiral Poulett, and the title and estates of Earl Poulett of Hinton St. George in the county of Somerset. William Poulett had been educated at Sandhurst, and was an officer in the 2nd Queen's Royal Regiment of Foot. He was a drinking, racing, betting man, a good fellow in most senses of the word. On board ship, with his fellow officers, in cheerful mood, one of his bets was said to have been that he would marry the first girl he saw from the windows of the mess, when he landed in England. The story has a ring of truth, although there are other versions.

The facts were that he married the daughter of a pilot from Landport in Dorset on 23 June 1849. She was presumably a pretty girl and pleasing to the gallant officer. But there was one small fact which she had concealed – she was pregnant by another man, a certain Captain William Turnour Greville. William Poulett had been made a scapegoat to give the child a name. When she confessed the facts of her situation, Ensign Poulett left her. He refused either to support, or to acknowledge the child although he made his wife an allowance. The son of Elizabeth Lavinia Poulett née Newman was born on 15 December 1849, some six months after the marriage. Poulett never saw his wife or her child again. He had married her on 23 June, but had left her on the 8 August. The marriage had lasted less than two months.

William Poulett decided to forget his folly by serving abroad, and exchanged into the 22nd Regiment of Foot and sailed for India. Here Poulett served with distinction, and received a medal and clasp for the storming of the Boree Pass under General Boileau. India also gave him the chance to indulge in his other passion – racing. While he was in the North Western Provinces he rode in fifty-seven races, winning forty-three of them. He did not return from India until

1855, and continued to be a gallant serving officer, and racing man until 1857. Then the whole picture of his life changed.

His uncle, the Earl Poulett, had three sons. One died in 1843, the year of William Poulett's rash marriage. In 1857 his cousin Amias, who had served with great bravery at the siege of Sebastopol, came back to his family home at Hinton St. George in Somerset – and suddenly died. In the same year the eldest brother, a colonel in the Somerset militia took to his bed in his home in Dover Street – and he also died. The following year, William's father the Admiral died, and William had become heir to his uncle, the Earl Poulett of Hinton House, Hinton St. George in the County of Somerset.

The old Earl, foreseeing trouble with the unacknowledged child of Elizabeth Newman, tied up the estate on any heirs to be subsequently declared legitimate. He was taking no risks when it came to the dashing Captain Poulett, and the future of Hinton St. George.

On learning of his possible inheritance, the captain sold his commission and decided to devote himself to his second love – racing. He bought an estate in Hampshire, and settled down. Not to a second marriage, but to breeding horses, training horses, and riding to hounds as Master of the Hambledon Hunt on his favourite

The 6th Earl Poulett, Master of the Hambledon Hunt. Portrait by Harry Hall

mare Irish Molly. It was said that 'at no period since their existence had the hounds been so liberally managed'.

He was nicely placed at Grenville Hall for his twin hobbies, horses and yachting. He became known in racing circles all over the country and on the Continent – famous for boldness in hunting, racing, and sailing. His friend and crony, with whom he lived, was George Ede, a famous amateur sportsman who had ridden 300 winners, sometimes against professional jockeys, and who had founded the Hampshire Cricket Club. William Poulett had some-one to share his interests. While there were horses to be ridden and raced, the marriage stakes was a race he did not choose to risk again.

In 1864 the old Earl died, and the gallant and sporting captain became Earl Poulett. But by 1864 he had been for seven years totally devoted to racing and hunting at Grenville Hall in the County of Hampshire. When a man had a good pack of hounds and a racing stud what was the point of moving to Hinton St. George? Besides there was always the chance of winning the Grand National, for George Ede had found a horse called The Lamb, in Ireland.

The Lamb stood only fourteen or fifteen hands, and had been much despised at his first sale, knocked down at twenty-five guineas as not being 'big enough to carry a man's boots'. But Ede and Earl Poulett had seen something they liked about the horse. Ede particu-larly, who had ridden in six Grand Nationals without success, saw the possibility that The Lamb could be his chance to win at last.

Just before the race Ede fell when hurdle racing, and was carried back covered in his own blood. But though bloodied, George Ede was totally unbowed and still determined to ride The Lamb in the National.

On the great day a gale sprang up. The Lamb, quoted at ten to one, soon went into the lead. His rival runner, Chimney Sweep, broke a leg and had to be shot. The race was so gruelling that only three horses finished, but first was The Lamb, ridden by George Ede, two lengths in front at the finishing post. By this time the gale was at full force, marquees were blown down, looters sacked the wreckage, the police were called in to quell a minor riot, but the congratulations went on. George and the Earl were toasting their success while the gale raged outside.

Six years later, in 1870, George Ede was riding in the Sefton Chase at Liverpool when his mount, Chippenham, fell and rolled on his rider. George Ede was dragged along with his foot caught in the stirrup. He died as he had lived – for racing. A great partnership had ended, but the horse Ede had found still lived, and in 1871 Poulett had two dreams. As was natural for this sporting gentleman, they were both about racing.

He wrote to the champion jockey, Pickernell, who rode under the name of 'Mr. Thomas'.

My dear Tommy,

Let me know for certain whether you can ride for me at Liverpool on The Lamb. I dreamt twice last night I saw the race. The first dream he was last and finished amongst the carriages. The second dream, I should think an hour afterwards I saw The Lamb run. He won by four lengths, and *you* rode him, and I saw the cerise and blue sleeves and you, as plain as I write this. Now let me know as soon as you can, and say nothing to anyone.

Yours sincerely,

Poulett.

Over-excited by his dream, and the fact that Pickernell had accepted to ride, Poulett forgot all about the necessity for secrecy and began sending out circulars to all his friends urging them to bet on a certainty.

The omens were good, the day was fair and bright. A public holiday had been declared in honour of the marriage of Princess Louise, daughter of Queen Victoria, to the Marquess of Lorne. The crowds were large, estimated to be nearly 50,000, and one of Poulett's horses, Broadlea, reckoned to be an also-ran, had won the Molyneux Chase the day before. Rumours were rife. A live lamb had been seen running across the race course. Another had been spotted at the railway station.

The excitement was such that some racegoers ran on to the course after the start, and were charged by the leading runners being knocked down 'like ninepins, with severe injury to some'. But the race went on. At the end of the first circuit, fifteen out of twenty-five runners were gone. At the Canal turn The Lamb had lost the advantage, but carried on gamely. Two more horses fell in front of him, but he jumped the mêlée and finished first by two lengths from Despatch. Souvenir hunters pulled most of the hairs out of the tail of The Lamb. It was the horse's moment of glory never to be repeated. He was sold to Baron Oppenheim for £1,200 and taken to Germany.

But already other aspects of Earl Poulett's life were casting a shadow. In 1870 William Henry Turnour, son of Elizabeth Newman, the Earl's wife, became twenty-one and decided to go down to Somerset to inspect his hoped-for inheritance. He stayed at the George Hotel in Crewkerne, and grandly hired a trap in which he was driven in great style to Hinton St. George. William Turnour had become a tall, handsome young man, and was dressed in the height of fashion as became the heir to Hinton House and the title of Earl Poulett, as he now claimed.

The 6th Earl was temporarily installed at Hinton St. George but quite as set against the young man as he had been before his birth. In the days before blood tests, claims to earldoms were not so easily disproved. But the Earl had no hesitation. He had been duped by a light woman, and was in no mood to accept the young man as his heir. He ordered his servants to have William Turnour turned away from the gates. When the Earl heard that a local innkeeper had refreshed the young man with a glass of beer, he promptly cancelled the pub keeper's lease, and had him turned out of the village.

It was correctly reported that Earl Poulett had offered the claimant £800 a year to cease bothering him, and to give up all claim to the estate and title of Viscount Hinton. This William Turnour refused to do, which was probably the reason for the Earl's anger. Oddly enough the Dowager Duchess of Cleveland was more sympathetic to the young man, and occasionally helped him with money, but there is no evidence that she accepted his claims.

Turnour had been educated at Church House College in Merton where he had learned to speak French fluently. Like many others of personable appearance and pleasing voice, he decided to go on the stage. He began as a singer, and in 1869 he married a ballet dancer named Lydia Ann Shippy. She was the daughter of one William Shippy, described as a 'general dealer', which could have been a polite name for a rag-and-bone man. It was presumably his marriage, and possibly his wife, which had pushed William Turnour into visiting the Earl and trying to claim his inheritance in 1870.

The following year in 1871, Elizabeth Newman, 6th Countess Poulett was dying in lodgings in Portsmouth. Her husband, although adamant about not acknowledging her son, had supported her in modest circumstances. When she was mortally ill, her son visited her to find out if she needed anything. She whispered that she lacked nothing, but added: 'There is an eye sometimes stares through that crack in the door that troubles me.'

William reassured her; it was, he thought, a dying woman's fancy. But his mother insisted. She had seen the eye too frequently for it to be her imagination. Worried about the hallucination, as he thought it to be, William asked the landlady. Was there anyone who came to spy on his sick mother?

The landlady looked at him. 'Yes, it is true. Emma Johnson comes down from Rosebank, Waterloo, to find out how soon your mother is going to die, and she has peeped through the door.'

Elizabeth Newman died on 9 August 1871 almost exactly twenty-two years since her husband had left her after their very brief marriage. A few weeks later on 20 September 1871, Earl Poulett married Emma Johnson, the lady with the watching eye. But Emma did not achieve her ambition to produce the rightful heir, and five years later, in 1876, she died without issue. On her monument the Earl described her as a 'gentle affectionate and truly loved wife', a statement which seems to accord ill with the landlady's story.

But the claimant William Turnour had not given up his pretensions. In 1872, one of the local newspapers reported: 'Earl Poulett's son and heir visited the village of Hinton St. George, and spent the night at Lord Westbury's at Hinton House'. Presumably the Earl's tenants had accepted the claimant as the rightful heir. Church bells were rung in his honour and flags put out around the village, and even the local pub, the Poulett Arms, was decorated with bunting. In the absence of the sporting Earl, the villagers, including the innkeeper, were prepared to risk his anger. Possibly another thought in their minds was that *if* William Turnour did become the 7th Earl, it was as well to be friendly before the event.

Although William Turnour had refused the Earl's offer of £800 a year to renounce his claims, no doubt, like the Earl with his Grand National winner, he felt he was on to a certainty. In the ensuing years things did not augur well for the claimant. His stage career foundered. His voice failed and he took engagements as a comedian. He became a clown at the Surrey Theatre, cavorting under the name of Mr. Cosman. He does not seem to have been particularly appreciated as a funny man, but his marriage proved more fruitful than his career. By Lydia, William had three children, a son William born in 1870, and two girls. These children were helped by the sympathetic Duchess of Cleveland, who had the girls educated in a French convent, and eventually left the boy £5,000 in her will.

On 1 March 1879 at the age of fifty-two, Earl Poulett was married for the third time to Rosa de Melville, daughter of an artist Hugh de Melville. It was a happy marriage, and the Earl was at last provided with an heir. On 11 September 1883, his legitimate son William John Lydston Poulett, the Viscount Hinton, was born at 30 Belsize Park Gardens in London.

By this time the villagers at Hinton had presumably decided against the claimant because the birth of William John Lydston was greeted with more bunting and ringing of church bells. The Earl entertained 2,000 guests in his grounds and gave a rich dinner to celebrate the event. Whether the offending innkeeper who had given the claimant a glass of beer was forgiven by this time is not recorded. Perhaps all had been pardoned in the general rejoicing. Speeches of fulsomeness and gratitude were made. One man described the Earl as 'a thorough man of business who saw in a moment what his tenants wanted and why they wanted it. He never said "no" to their desires if he could possibly help it, and if he was obliged to say "no" he did it in *such* a pleasant way that the denial was given without the tenant feeling it.' Another tenant, inspired by his Lordship's good wine, announced that he could not say enough in praise of the Earl. He had shown kindness and condescension to one and all, and the speaker was sure that all present could say the same. This statement was greeted with huzzahs for his Lordship, the landlord.

None of this junketing deterred William Turnour who still maintained that he was the rightful heir. By 1889 he had lost all chance of stage success and was pushing a barrel-organ round his native Southsea with a placard on top. On this was written in bold letters: 'I am Viscount Hinton, eldest son of Earl Poulett, I have adopted this as a means of earning a living, my father having refused to assist me through no fault of my own.'

In the summer months when the ships were full of trippers, Turnour earned a precarious living by playing his barrel-organ for their entertainment as the steamers plied between Dover and Calais. The French newspapers took up his story, and printed a cartoon of the organ-grinder, winding the handle of his organ, wearing ragged clothes, and on his head sat an outsize coronet. About 1890 Turnour and his wife moved to Islington and here he continued to ply his trade in the grey streets of London.

In the same year, when Viscount Hinton was seven years old, the Earl brought an action which was called 'Perpetuation of Testimony', in which he plainly stated the facts as to why William Turnour had no claims on him in view of the dates of the marriage and of Turnour's birth. The Earl himself was a witness, but the case was not conclusive, and while the Earl continued in good health, the matter did not seem to be one of urgency.

In 1895 the sporting Earl fell into financial difficulties. His sporting activities had not added to his income and his rents were much depleted by the agricultural depression. The estate was put into the hands of receivers. Two years later in 1899 Earl Poulett died and his sixteen-year-old son succeeded him, but the shadow of the claimant still lay over him.

William Turnour, by this time, was living in a slum tenement, 17 Henry Buildings, Penton Street, Islington.

The day after the village bells had been rung to announce the melancholy news of the Earl's death, reporters were in the street interviewing 'Viscount Hinton' on his pitch at Upper Street, Islington. He was turning the barrel-organ handle, as one newspaper cartoon put it, 'in an haristocratic way', while his wife collected coppers thrown by passers-by.

The interview was conducted with mock solemnity by the reporter:

'Viscount Hinton, I believe?'

'I am he.'

'I have to inform you that Earl Poulett died yesterday at his town house 60 Queen's Gate.'

'Do you really mean that?'

'Yes.'

'Then I am Earl Poulett.'

The report continued: 'The news when fully grasped, seemed to stun the recipient. He could hardly realise that, at last, after years of humiliation, he stood once more with a chance of regaining the position to which he had looked forward for so long. His wife, who walked painfully with a stick, seemed to adapt herself more quickly to her dignity: "I am sorry to hear that the Earl is dead, but William, I am heartily grateful that your troubles are over at last." '

The report underlined the drama of the scene which took place in the roar and hum of the Islington traffic. The supposed Earl reacted swiftly to his new honours. 'Come with me, and we'll talk about it,' he said to the reporter, and then he said: 'But first, I must pack the machine up.' The old man who helped to drag the organ home at night was rewarded with money to buy himself half a pint.

Away from the traffic 'Earl Poulett' was asked what he felt. 'I hardly know – it is certainly unexpected, and I may say, frankly, welcome, for though I have not wished the death of my father, despite the manner in which he has treated me, I am glad, at last, I shall be placed beyond the sordid existence I have been obliged to lead. I shall, of course, take immediate steps, through my solicitors, to assert my claim to the title and entailed estate.'

'Will there not be opposition from the family?'

'Yes, I dare say there will be some opposition on the part of the family. My father leaves a wife, his third, and I think three other children – a boy and two girls, but I do not think there is any doubt about my right of succession. Of course, the income from the property is greatly reduced owing to the involved state of the late Earl's affairs, as the result of which his rents have been estreated during the past year or more to the benefit of his creditors.'

William Turnour had been keeping up with the news of his 'father' and also keeping a sharp eye on what had happened to his affairs.

'What the amount of the inheritance will be is therefore impossible to say at present,' said the 'Earl' grandly. 'but at any rate I should receive an income which will enable me to live in comparative luxury. Of course, I shall discard my barrel-organ at once. It would hardly look the thing for an Earl Poulett to play in the streets, would it?'

He explained his appearance to his interviewers; it was unfortunate that he should be so shabby at this moment of his life, but his rooms had been broken into and some thief had taken all his wardrobe, including five frock coats.

'What do you intend to do now?'

'I shall certainly call on my solicitors first thing in the morning.'

And then, like so many men and women who spend their lives in hopes and projected lawsuits, he went back to his tenement to 'look through his papers'.

The day after his interview another reporter called at 17 Henry Buildings and this time the 'Earl' was out seeing his solicitors, and the 'Countess' was interviewed. She was sadly frank.

'I am not sorry that there is a prospect of our street life being ended. Since I injured my ankle I have not been able to assist in pulling the organ, and William has been poorly for some time. He suffers from rheumatism in the legs and very often he is unable to stand. But I have stuck to him all these years, and I would have stuck to him to the end in any case.'

She admitted that many times they had been in sore straits, sometimes half-starved. 'But we would have starved rather than take the assistance that the late Earl sent indirectly through policemen and others.'

The 'Countess' said she had been married to 'Viscount Hinton' for twenty-eight years and, although there had been little romance in their circumstances, it had been one of 'those cases of love at first sight between them'.

'We have lived very happily,' she said, adding fondly: 'Willie is so good tempered. We have three children – two girls and one boy. Our son was left £5,000 by the Duchess of Cleveland, and is now in Ceylon engaged as a teaplanter. The girls are in a French convent.'

At the end of the interview the claimant arrived home, and in fighting mood. Although his solicitor had told him that there was little hurry in pushing his suit, 'I am determined,' he declared, 'to go down to Hinton St. George – my property and take possession!'

'Do you anticipate any opposition?'

'I do not!'

'What if opposition is offered?'

'I will do what I did one time before – I will break down the gates

– and enter! It was some time in the seventies that I resorted to that. Along with a friend named Billy Blorr I was in the vicinity of Hinton St. George. I wanted to get into the park that is part of my possessions, and I was informed by one of my father's servants that it was a right of way. With very little ceremony I cut down the gates, placed them under St. George's cross – and walked in!'

The battling 'Earl' went on: 'If there is any legal fighting to be done, I shan't shirk it. My case is clear. Those for the Hon. William John Lydston have to establish theirs.'

The reporter then touched on the delicate matter of his mother's frailty. 'Was it not true that your father married your mother after a few days' acquaintance?'

'As a matter of fact,' said the 'Earl', 'they lived together at least two years before they were married.'

Perhaps this had been William Turnour's mother's story. She had lived with a man for two years before she married – but it had not been William Poulett.

'The banns were published at Landport,' said the 'Earl', and added that in due form, three weeks after the publication of the banns, his parents had been married. There was no doubt about it, he was born in wedlock.

'Was it not true that soon after the wedding your parents separated?' asked the reporter.

'Yes. But my mother had been provided with a good income – which died with her.'

'What about you?'

'My father did not provide for me. He did make an offer but it was on the condition that I dropped the title and went to a distant part. If I complied, he was to settle £800 a year on me. I refused!'

A man had his pride – and his expectations.

'I then took to theatrical life, the Dowager Duchess of Cleveland assisting me greatly.'

'When did you first take to organ-grinding?'

'It must have been about 1889. My first pitch was on the beach of my native Southsea.'

He admitted that he had had a hard life, but now it was all over. He intended to take his seat in the House of Lords.

The interviewer then asked the classic question: 'When did you last see your father?'

'About two months ago, when I was playing the organ in the Brompton Road. He did not recognise me.'

William Turnour was now fifty and broken in health by frustrated hopes, but once more the glimmering grail of title and estates appeared before his eyes.

104

The old Earl had died on 22 January 1899 and his body was taken with due ceremony from London to Somerset three days later. On the coffin of polished oak lay a scarlet and gold cushion and on the cushion the coronet so much coveted by William Turnour, of Henry's Buildings, Pentonville.

Tenants and parishioners filed meekly past to pay their last respects to their late Lord. The church was filled with the perfume of the many wreaths, and when the service was over the estate workers carried the remains of the sporting Earl to the family vault. The ceremonies were traditional and carried out with that respect due to the status of the dead man.

Only one person was missing at the funeral – the claimant, William Turnour. He had been unable to attend owing to an accident while pushing his barrel-organ along Rosebery Avenue. The *Daily Telegraph* decided that such a human story was worth pursuing.

It was not difficult to find the buildings, but this particular set of apartments occupied by the aristocratic street musician required diligent search owing to the scarcity of light in this particular quarter of Pentonville. The presence of a stranger soon attracted a crowd of small boys who swarmed round the 'buildings'.

'I guess you're looking for the Viscount,' said one.

'He's no Viscount he's a bloomin' Lord now. If you want to see his lawdship, you goes along this dark passage up those stairs to number 17, and mind you don't break your bloomin' neck on the way. Lights is scarce in Henry's Buildings.'

The man from the *Daily Telegraph* found William Turnour reclining on a horsehair sofa in a small back parlour; his room was scrupulously clean but poorly furnished. It was lighted by a small paraffin lamp, for it was a dark January morning.

The 'Viscount' is a man of presentable appearance, respectably clothed, and neither in demeanour nor conversation does he resemble those other organ-grinders who may be found any day in the purlieus of Saffron Hill.

He was surrounded by neighbours, attracted by the excitement of Turnour's apparent elevation to the peerage. When the reporter arrived, a middle-aged woman who had already taken on the role of housekeeper to the new Lord ushered the neighbours from the room. 'His Lordship *is* indisposed', she said to the reporter, 'but he will see you now.'

The claimant spoke with dignity to the *Daily Telegraph*. 'I am very glad to see you. I am not so badly hurt as they make out, and I hope to be out again soon. The fact is, I was going along Rosebery Avenue yesterday afternoon when I twisted my ankle. That's why I am stretched out here. But I can't complain, for I have plenty to interest me.'

He pointed to a small table upon which there was a huge pile of letters. There were letters on the mantelpiece, letters on the sofa and letters on the floor.

'Where did they all come from?' asked the reporter.

'From all parts of England, Ireland and Scotland. What's more they all breathe the same message – congratulations and sympathy. I value them all, but those from the poor touch me most. For years I have lived amongst poverty and I know how warm are the hearts of the poor.'

William Turnour read out a letter which was signed 'A poor old woman'; she had been a domestic at Hinton St. George and wrote that she had often thought the Earl should have allowed the claimant 'an annuity out of the lovely estate'. Dozens of other letters voiced the same sentiments. A sudden fortune is a dream realised for those without one.

The claimant admitted that his future plans were uncertain. 'My solicitor is acting for me.' Then he had a moment of doubt: 'If things go to the bad – there is always the piano organ. It is in a stable close by – and is in good condition.'

The interview was at an end. 'Good evening, Lord Hinton,' said the reporter.

'I beg your pardon, I am now Earl Poulett.'

Numbers of reporters visited the 'Earl' and rumours abounded. He was going to be paid off by the family – offers had been made. Syndicates were being formed to fight for his inheritance. Money was being raised amongst the tenants and farmers on the Hinton estate. Other moneys were forthcoming in the city where hard-headed men were backing the 'Earl's' claim. But the 'Earl' himself, when interviewed, was adamant that none of these stories was true. There was no question of a compromise and as far as he was concerned he was being guided completely by his lawyer, Mr. Hall. 'We have not one atom of doubt as to the justice and validity of our claims and we shall pursue strictly legal and orthodox methods.'

'And if you succeed?'

'If I succeed, I have but one ambition – to do good to the poor. As you know I have been in sore straits during the many years of my life and I know how tightly the shoe of poverty pinches. It would be my hobby to relieve as much suffering as possible. You little know how much of suffering there is in the country, and how patient the poor generally are. I am not an ambitious man, and have seen enough of the world in my time to estimate its tinsel and hollow glories at their true worth. I believe more in the substance than the shadow and I can assure you that I would esteem it a greater privilege to entertain a few poor families at a good dinner than to take my seat in the House of Lords. One more word in conclusion, you can tell the people who have said that I intend to break down the barriers at Hinton that they are talking bunkum. We want British law, not brute force.'

After a few months the excitement caused by the Earl's death and the possibilities of the organ-grinder moving in as the life tenant of Hinton House died down. The unfortunate organ-grinder went back to his pitch, and fell once more into obscurity, although he continued just as doggedly to pursue his claim.

At last on 27 May 1903 four years after the Earl's death *The Times* announced that Rosa Countess Poulett widow of William Henry Poulett, 6th Earl Poulett guardian of her son William John Lydston was petitioning that His Majesty declare that 'the said William John Lydston Poulett is by right entitled to the dignities and honours of Viscount Hinton of Hinton St. George and Earl Poulett'. The petition was referred to the Committee of Privileges. After due deliberation, the late Earl's evidence of 1890 was re-examined. On 31 July 1903 their Lordships reached a verdict. The Lord Chancellor gave the decision:

Before her marriage with the late Earl, the latter's wife, Elizabeth Lavinia née Newman admitted misconduct with Captain Granville, and after the marriage she made an admission to her husband to that effect.

The report went on to say that the Earl had behaved in such a way as to make it plain that he was not the father of the child. Their Lordships had done some ferreting amongst the movements of the late Earl's regiment, and no doubt some medical counting on their fingers, and they had come up with the firm belief that the regiment was not in England at the time of William Turnour's conception. The conclusion was:

There was no doubt that the claimant was illegitimate. ... The Lord Chancellor moved that it would be the duty of their Lordships to report to the House that the claimant, the son of Elizabeth Lavinia Poulett, had not made out his claim and that the counter-claimant had. Their Lordships agreed.

William Turnour may have said he preferred substance to shadow, it was not true. He preferred hope to hard cash.

The villagers of Hinton St. George once more decorated their village with flags and bunting and rang the church bells. Perhaps there were still a few old cottagers who remembered that once upon a time the village had been decorated for the false claimant, but all that was forgotten. When the young Earl arrived back in the village the horses were unharnessed from his carriage and he was dragged in triumph to Hinton House.

Two years later there were further celebrations when the Earl came of age at twenty-one. The estate had been carefully administered during his minority and was more than solvent. A dinner was given for the tenants, and his young Lordship gave the toast: 'Foxhunting, hare-hunting, and general sports!' This was well received especially by the Master of Seavington Hunt who fulsomely replied. The tenants had had a whip round for their landlord and a large piece of plate was presented with their good wishes, and there was a long speech from the oldest tenant of the estate, William Penny of Combe Farm. He ended by saying that one and all would be proud to present another piece of plate when his young Lordship should choose to bring home a bride to Hinton House. The gift was handed over. It was appropriately a silver statuette of his Lordship in hunting costume, surrounded by his pack of hounds.

To the happiness of village and estate, in 1908 the 7th Earl Poulett did bring back a bride to Hinton St. George; she was Sylvia Storey, one of the prettiest girls from the Gaiety chorus. She was just eighteen.

Sylvia Storey was the daughter of Fred Storey, a scene painter and eccentric dancer. Her father exercised his talent for dancing mostly in pantomime, the medium in which the poor organ-grinder had failed. Although he made his living on the stage, Fred Storey had a middle class and artistic background. His uncle was G. A. Storey, a painter, and Royal Academician, and his great-uncle had been G. P. Harley, well-known as an actor on the Victorian stage.

Sylvia herself began her career at the age of twelve in the Seymour Hicks play *Bluebell in Fairyland*, playing Annie, one of the romanticised flower girls. There were pictures in the Press of the child actors being instructed in their time off to prove that no one was exploiting their charm and innocence. Good was also seen to be done for other little boys and girls who were perhaps not so comfortably placed as the juvenile players or their audience.

The programme announced: 'A collecting box will be found in the vestibule for the Fresh Air Fund, and *The Referee* Children's Dinner Fund. Your Pennies will be welcomed.'

Countess Poulett
formerly Miss Sylvia
Storey, daughter of Mr.
Fred Storey, the well-
known comedian

The 7th Earl Poulett

Home Notes was running the story of the play, and the programme also informed the children 'if any little boy or girl would like to have the story bound in cloth and gold, they should write to Aunt Hilda of *Home Notes* saying what they had seen at the Pantomime, and how they enjoyed it. Aunt Hilda will then send to ten little girls named Mary, and ten little boys named John, a copy of the book' – which was bad luck for those not called John or Mary.

Sylvia continued to play in musical comedy, and in 1907, just before she met Earl Poulett, she was one of the 'guests' in the Seymour Hicks musical play *The Gay Gordons* set against a Scottish background. The scenes gave the ladies of the chorus a chance for several changes of costume. 'A moor in the Highlands' featured the girls, sportively clad in kilts, feathered bonnets, wearing boots and carrying guns. 'Tent in the Gardens of Melrose Castle' (afternoon dresses and garden party hats), 'Ballroom at Melrose Castle' (provocatively decolletée dresses, and the full toilette with jewels and flowers).

In the pictures of the chorus, Sylvia Storey stands out as the prettiest of the girls, with classically chiselled features, dark hair, large eyes, and a figure to enhance even the over-decorated costumes of the period.

The Gay Gordons opened in September of 1907, and in June of 1908 Sylvia met Earl Poulett. They were married quietly at St.

Chorus of *The Gay Gordons*. Sylvia Storey second from left, front row

110

James's, Piccadilly on 2 September 1908, and Lord Poulett brought his Countess to Hinton St. George a month later. Triumphal arches appeared all over the village. There were so many that prizes were offered for the most outstanding. Mottoes in flowers were everywhere. 'A hearty welcome home from All', 'God Bless the Happy Pair!', 'Hinton St. George Reading Room offer Warmest Greetings', 'May they prosper', 'East West, Home's Best', and across the gates to the mansion an archway proclaimed: 'All Blessings and Joys attend you both', while the clock tower over the front door of the house announced 'Home Sweet Home'.

The new Countess must have felt that she was still playing in the last act of some musical comedy, except that this time she was the leading lady and not one of the 'guests'. There were processions, songs, flags and cheers as the car wound its way down the village street. The car stopped under one of the triumphal arches, and the Earl with his new Countess got out. Sylvia Storey, late of the Gaiety Theatre, but now Countess Poulett (dressed in a grey mole colour Directoire skirt with a frilly white blouse and felt hat, in matching mole colour) was immediately presented with a huge bouquet of pink carnations, lily of the valley and smilax and fern tied with a pink satin bow. No sooner had she kissed the head keeper's little step-daughter who had presented the flowers, than the local schoolchildren struck up a 'Song of Welcome'. Headed by a rider in hunting dress, schoolchildren, villagers, village bands, and tenants then followed the slow progress of the car to the house. When night fell the whole village was illuminated with fairy lights and Chinese lanterns.

So Sylvia was welcomed home to Hinton House and took possession as châtelaine. Less than a year later an heir was born to the young couple – George Amias Fitzwarrine Poulett, Viscount Hinton. In 1912 a sister Lady Bridget Poulett completed the family.

But in that same year of 1912, the claimant William Turnour, self-styled Earl Poulett, died in the workhouse at the age of fifty-nine. Unlike his mother's husband the 6th Earl, he had not backed a winner.

HEARTSEASE
or
Moss vs. Earl Compton (later
Marquess of Northampton)

❦❦❦❦❦❦❦❦❦❦❦❦❦❦❦❦❦❦❦❦❦❦❦❦❦❦❦❦

When Daisy Markham (Mrs. Moss) met Earl Compton in 1912, she was acting in *The Glad Eye*. Daisy, a dark-haired, dark-eyed young woman of twenty-five was playing Suzanne Polignac, the artless and confiding wife of an errant husband. Daisy was accustomed to play artless girls. She had been the *ingénue* in Maugham's *The Tenth Man*, in *Love Watches*, and *Leah Kleschna* (with Lena Ashwell). Her roles demanded that she should look soft and charming in a series of fetching toilettes which set off her slim figure. Feathered hats, jewels, and flounced dresses showed her off to advantage in a series of parts so small that she was seldom mentioned – except in the cast list. *The Glad Eye* appears to have been her greatest success on the London stage, and in that piece she was noticed as 'making the most of the opportunities afforded her'.

This classic French farce abounded in guilty husbands hiding in cupboards when they were supposed to be off ballooning, a tough wife blackmailing her faithless husband for a set of sables, and the faithful wife (Daisy) refusing the advances of the husband's friend: 'M. Floquet, I like you very much – as a *friend*, but I assure you, you're only wasting your time making love to me – I haven't the slightest intention of deceiving my husband.'

Daisy, as Suzanne, uttered these innocent words looking gentle and sweet, with a posy of simple flowers pinned to her shoulder as she arranged a bowl of roses on an occasional table.

The *Daily Telegraph* wasn't taken in by all this superficial simplicity, and took care to warn its readers of possible moral damage, for although the piece was funny, it was necessary to handle it with care. '*The Glad Eye* occasionally hovers on the borderland of indiscretion, for José Levey has failed to remove all traces of the play's birthplace, but if the listener be prepared to leave the "*dessous des cartes*" unexamined he will come to no harm.'

112

Daisy had been on the stage since the age of eighteen. The biography which she gave to *Who's Who in The Theatre* in 1912, the year she met Earl Compton, noted that she was born in India, her father being Charles Markham and her mother Lydia Finlay. There was no mention of the station in life of her parents, or of their occupations and it must be assumed that she preferred to keep her humble origins quiet. There was also no mention of her ex-husband Mr. Moss – presumably a piece of moss she had discarded early in her career.

At the time of their meeting, William Bingham, the Earl Compton, was the senior subaltern of the Royal Horse Guards, a young man about town, handsome and elegant, heir not only to Castle Ashby in Northamptonshire, but to Compton Wynyates, and the estate of Loch Luichart in Scotland. His ancestors (and the families of the women to whom they allied themselves) sound a roll-call of aristocracy and privilege: Ferrers, Egmonts, Leveson-Gowers; the Compton women also did not neglect to marry into the correct governing stream of society. Even Lord Compton's second name of 'Bingham' indicated an alliance into the family of Lord Ashburton, and the banking family of Baring; the first Lord Ashburton had married the daughter of William Bingham of Philadelphia, a Senator of the United States in the eighteenth century. So the

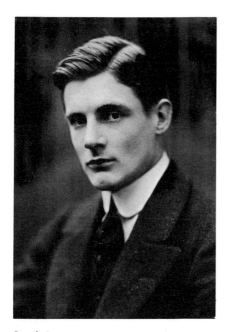

Lord Compton: young man about town

correct marriages of the Compton family stretched across the length and breadth of England and Scotland, and even across the Atlantic.

The Comptons were a very ancient family. William Compton (son of Edmund de Compton) was the first of the family to be knighted 'having been employed in his youth about the person of Henry VIII and obtained the confidence of that monarch'. Sir William Compton did not neglect his opportunities. He became Chief Gentleman of the Bedchamber, which was possibly no sinecure under Henry VIII. He collected well-paid posts from his royal master, fought in his battles, and attended him at the Field of the Cloth of Gold. Although he had estates all over England, when he decided to marry he chose a lady with some estates of her own. Prudent marriages set the pattern for the Compton family for the next 350 years. Even to young Earl Compton it must have seemed a long way from the Field of the Cloth of Gold to *The Glad Eye* at the Globe Theatre. He had a hard task before him. It was one thing to dash about London accompanied by a pretty young actress in an expensive motor car, and promise eternal fidelity, and quite another to approach father in his Elizabethan mansion and get permission to marry the girl. Lord Compton was a demon driver. He had already been fined several times for 'scorching', and on 1 May 1913, about the time when he had to confront his father, he was fined for driving a motor car in Rocks Lane, Barnes Common, at the excessive speed of thirty-two miles an hour. As the Leamar sisters sang:

> Go and inform your Father
> Wont he be angry – rather!
> Say how you feel
> Nothing to conceal
> So – go and inform your Dad!

The rest of the music-hall song contained a slur on the papas of the period: 'At Romano's – as Papa knows – the wines and the women are grand.'

Unfortunately for Lord Compton, his papa was not accustomed to frequent Romano's. His father was a distinguished man, who besides being a Knight of the Garter, and a Knight of Grace of the Order of St. John of Jerusalem, had been M.P. for South West Warwickshire. He was a pillar of the Church, had caused many churches on his estates to be repaired and restored, and, in addition, was President of the British and Foreign Bible Society. He was such an active member of that august body that he had put the circulation of bibles up from five million to eight million, and increased the

'At Romano's – as Papa knows – The wines and the women are grand'

number of languages in which the Bible was translated to over ninety.

He not only supported the Church, but he did a great deal of good to the deserving poor. He did not contemplate the broad avenue of trees from his windows, or the villages which he owned with complacency. Did the village of Yardley Hastings need a new water supply – he supplied it. Did his tenants in Northampton Square need a garden, he presented it. Were there slums to be cleared in the Clerkenwell district where he was ground landlord, he would be the first to put the idea forward. He was Chairman of the Housing Committee which cleared the Strand district of crumbling houses and rookeries, and built the Aldwych and Kingsway. When it was said of him that he never allowed himself to forget that property had its responsibilities as well as its duties, it was well said.

It can therefore be appreciated that when the dashing Earl Compton announced to his father his intention of marrying Miss Daisy Markham this news was ill received in the panelled halls of Castle Ashby. Comptons did not ally themselves with French farces, or form alliances with the Globe Theatre. Although Earl Compton did inform his dad, the answer which dad returned was that it was totally out of the question. Daisy must go.

So the wretched Lord Compton sat down in his ancestral home of Castle Ashby, gloomily contemplating its turrets with their improving mottoes in Latin: 'Except that the Lord Build the House, they labour in vain that build it.'

Castle Ashby

He gazed out of the window at the balustrade erected in honour of his mother: 'Consider the lilies of the field how they grow.' He was not considering the lilies, he was thinking of Daisy. But there was a job which had to be done; he commenced to write to his dearest Daisy. It was not an easy task. On the one hand there was his father religious, widowed, lonely, and in the graveyard, weeping stone angels mourning his dead mother. And on the other – the alluring picture of Daisy, chiffon veiling her girlish breast, a smile on her lips, and eyes which promised endless fun and fulfilment. How to tell her she must go? In a fine frenzy of passion he had promised her the earth – gracious living, Castle Ashby and Compton Wynyates, a home in Scotland, and above all a coronet on her sweet head. A dear head which he had filled with dreams of grandeur. How could he –

116

cad that he was – snatch all this way and leave his dear girl feeling that he loved her all the same?

He dipped his pen into the silver inkpot, and wrote. Dearest Daisy – like Christopher Robin he knew that was right. But how to go on? How to express the choking hopeless sensation he felt at losing a life of passion with the luscious Daisy? She was his ideal, he wrote. Maybe she would find it hard to believe in his love, but it was equally hard to face the ways of a harsh world.

Daisy must realise that he was only doing it all from a sense of duty, and trying to think for *both* of them. He pondered darkly on that thought. Darling, sweet little Daisy, so soft, so yielding, and above all loving *him* so much she would understand. He again expressed to her, not only his love, but his esteem and admiration. Parting was not only sweet sorrow for him, but in the long sad race of life it might be best for Daisy and her heartbroken Bim. It was a thought which even Bim, in his more lucid moments, realised might have little appeal for Daisy. There must be disadvantages, he would have to point these out to her. Other women – that was the ticket – other women might treat her badly. She had no idea, he pointed out, of how real 'ladies' could behave. She would suffer humiliation and scorn. How could he, her loving Bimbo, stand idly by and see her pierced to the heart with the sneers of socialites, so much beneath her in beauty and brains? It would be agony for the sweet sensitive character of his dear darling Daisy, and even greater agony for her despairing Bimbo. He did not want to give her up, but what could he do?

His father's face calling him to the stern path of duty – backed up by the sale of eight million Bibles, translated into every language from Hindi to Swahili – glimmered sternly over the writing paper. The worst part of it for Bim was that his parent had only voiced his own secret views. It was all very well to promise eternal fidelity when clasped in the arms of a charming piece of womanhood, but the faces of all those ancestors who kept the honour of the family, and the main chance, well in view when it came to marriage, called him back to Compton common sense. He knew he had his position to think of. If only he could escape from that! He mentioned this thought to Daisy. Then he remembered the brief letter of dismissal he had written to her only that morning. She would think him a swine for being so direct. But he was demented between love and duty. Surely she could realise that? He felt there was nothing left to live for without his dearest Daisy. But how could he have written so brutally? He explained to her that he was compelled to beat down his reason. His heart was dead, and he now felt that he had cruelly wounded her. Could she – would she – forgive him? Yes – the dear old girl would understand. He pictured her understanding face as she heard how much he loved and respected her, and wished her all the pluck she would need, and ended by signing himself her broken hearted Bim.

He read the letter over, and it seemed to him to be not only heartbroken but loving – Daisy above all women would understand. . . . Unfortunately Daisy, dazzled by the prospect of several stately homes, a coronet, not to mention a coat of arms with a dragon (dexter), ducally gorged and chained or, and (sinister) a unicorn horned, maned, hoofed and tufted, was not so inclined to let all these glories depart with an *ingénue* smile. If anyone was going to be chained or, maned and tufted, it was going to be William Bingham, the Earl Compton. He had promised to marry her, and marry her he should.

Darling sweet little Daisy would understand

She had now received two letters telling her that her hopes of a glittering future as a marchioness were over. But if her broken hearted Bimbo was relying on her sweet sensitive nature, he was sadly mistaken. Nor did he have to wish her all the pluck she would need. If anyone was determined not to let her heart conquer her head it was dearest Daisy. The despairing Bimbo may have imagined a sad tear-stained letter from his ideal woman, followed perhaps by some expensive little parting gift from himself. This was not at all Daisy's idea of her future. She had a number of letters from her heartbroken Bimbo, promising her marriage and these, if they could not gain her a coronet, could at least be used to secure her some kind of future.

She decided to let the unhappy Bim stew in his own juice, and took action. She consulted lawyers – the best lawyers – and in the way of good lawyers, they put her in touch with the best barristers; for ex-Mrs. Moss (stage name Daisy Markham) nothing but the best would suffice. Sir Edward Carson, K.C., Mr. Hemmerde, K.C., Mr. McCardie and Mr. Costello were briefed to seek financial balm for her broken heart. She had all the evidence of breach of promise, she had the lawyers, and she was out for the kill.

On the other side were ranged Mr. Duke K.C. and Mr. F. E. Smith K.C. (afterwards Lord Birkenhead). The battle was joined, and the legal brains were prepared, like Tweedledum and Tweedledee, for a splendid and spectacular battle.

Lord Compton's father, having made his position clear on the question of marriage, left England to take the cure at Acqui. Acqui was one of those large spas which had sprung up during late Victorian times, full of over-decorated hotels which clustered round the healing waters of a life-giving spring. They were the health farms of Victorian and Edwardian days. Here the Marquess proposed to recuperate. He was suffering from rheumatism and no doubt was looking forward to the soothing attentions of masseuses, bath attendants, and well-trained staff at his hotel. He had been a widower for more than ten years. His heir was giving him nothing but trouble, it would be pleasant to relax and enjoy the medical pleasures of Acqui.

On the night before he left for Italy, the Marquess had addressed a meeting in London on behalf of the Northampton Training Ship Scheme. He arrived at the springs on the following day – and died of heart failure.

On 17 June, *The Times* announced his death.

We regret to announce that the Marquess of Northampton died suddenly on Sunday night at Acqui, Italy at the age of sixty-two.

He went to Italy to take a cure at Acqui for arthritis in a hip joint which was making him lame in the right leg.

William George Spencer Scott Compton succeeded to the titles of Marquess of Northampton, Earl of Northampton, Earl Compton of Compton and Baron Wilmington of Wilmington in Sussex in 1897.

The Times then went on sonorously to record his good deeds, his diplomatic career, and all the honours he had received.

The coffin was treated with the greatest ceremony all across Europe (for the late Marquess had been appointed Special Ambassador to the Courts of France, Italy and Greece to announce the accession of George V), crossed the Channel and was received with deep obeisances at Dover.

By the time it arrived at Castle Ashby for the funeral, the flags of Italy, France and Britain covered it. Waiting bareheaded at Castle Ashby station were Bim, now the Marquess of Northampton, with his sister Lady Loch, and his brother Lord Spencer Douglas Compton. The family had reclaimed the errant Bim, and his responsibilities lay before him.

A special message of sympathy arrived from King George V who was represented at the funeral by Lord Ashby St. Ledgers. *The Times* duly recorded the eminent people who assembled to mourn the late Marquess – Spencers, Comptons, Grahams, Leveson-Gowers, they were all there in force. Funerals and weddings bring the clans together, they give reassurance that the family ties hold firm in spite of mortality.

The Marquess had chosen to be buried amongst his own people and the service was conducted in the little village church adjacent to the house. The stone building was full of memorials, which enclosed the remains of dead Comptons, some simple, some pompous, and some sentimental. Behind the black-clad representative of the King and the family mourners, it was only fitting that the estate people should follow. The Marquess had always cared for them. The Guard of Honour was formed by the London Heavy Brigade of the Territorials.

But when the mourners had departed, and the mourning clothes had been put back into their mothballs, and the funeral wreaths had faded, there was another heavy brigade waiting for the unfortunate William Bingham, Marquess of Northampton, Earl of Northampton, Earl Compton of Compton, and Baron Wilmington of Wilmington (in Sussex); it was dearest Daisy.

Now that the despairing Bimbo had come into his extensive inheritance, Daisy felt herself entitled to richer pickings, and more substantial remuneration. Had things turned out differently she would now be loaded with family diamonds, and her dark head would have been crowned with a coronet or sparkling with a tiara. She was in no mood for mediation.

The new Marquess of Northampton, she felt, was hardly living up to his family motto: Je ne cherche que ung (I seek but one).

The Times reported the late Marquess's funeral on 23 June 1913, and on 2 July 1913, Daisy's case came up in the King's Bench Division, before Mr. Justice Bucknill and a special jury. Daisy's victim was now an extremely rich man, it was rumoured that his income was £150,000 a year, no mean sum in the days of the golden sovereign, when an excellent house could be bought for £200.

The court was packed with fashionable, and not so fashionable, people eager for succulent morsels of spicy scandal. Three hundred of them were standing in the well of the court, and the judge ordered all the gangways to be cleared. Many of those so eager for scandalous pickings were to be denied first hand knowledge of the proceedings.

Women reporters were much in evidence in the early 1900s. One of the programmes which has been preserved from Daisy's short theatrical career has a woman reporter's notes on her stage toilettes, scrawled illegibly on the page opposite the list of players. Daisy was obviously a lady who cared for fashion. Even when sitting at the court hearing her clothes were reported in detail.

'Miss Daisy Markham sat through the hearing, gazing as if in a dream at the soldierly figure of the young Marquess in front of her. She is petite and slim, and was becomingly attired in a fashionably-cut black satin costume, with a pink rosebud in the lapel of her jacket. Her only jewellery was a string of pearls round her neck; and she wore a hat trimmed with black-and-white chiffon.'

If there was one thing which must be admired about Daisy, it was her ability to dress suitably for the occasion. Subdued black and white proclaiming the death of love, and single rosebud indicating a tender heart.

A male reporter took a less romantic view of Miss Markham. 'In appearance she is petite and slim, with a pale complexion, full pouting lips, and arched eyebrows above eyes that look out at the beholder in a wide-eyed baby stare.' It was that wide-eyed baby stare which had gained her so many *ingénue* parts and had, like the Venus fly trap, attracted the dashing young Earl. But now that his father had been honourably interred in the family graveyard, he had perhaps come to see the parental point of view. Daisy was hardly suitable marchioness material.

The public and the Press were assembled in court; everyone

waited eagerly for salacious details to be thrown to their waiting jaws. Mr. McCardie (for Daisy) made a few opening remarks to the jury. Then a hurried consultation took place between Sir Edward Carson K.C. (also for Daisy), Mr. Duke for the now undespairing Bimbo (Marquess of Northampton), and their respective clients.

Sir Edward Carson rose impressively to address the Judge. He was happy to announce that he would not now have to enter into the details of the case. No doubt at this point an unhappy sigh escaped from the packed courtroom, from newspapermen and public alike. Were they to be cheated of their prey?

They were.

All that Sir Edward Carson said was that this was an action brought by Mrs. Moss (Daisy Markham) against the Earl Compton, as he was at the time of the engagement, now Marquess of Northampton. The parties met the previous year (1912). The promise of marriage followed which he understood was not denied. The defendant, afterwards, at the desire of his father, broke off the engagement, though he was fond of the lady, and in every way respected her, as was evident from the letter which he wrote, and which Mr. Duke had consented that he should read in court in order that there should be no misconception. Sir Edward then read the out-pourings of the despairing Bim, and added, in his dry legal way, 'The action was subsequently brought.'

He then went on to outline the way he had proceeded. He had most strongly advised the lady that, if possible, the matter should not be fought out to the bitter end as he believed that, in the interests of both parties, that was the wisest course. He had talked with Mr. Duke, and the Marquess of Northampton had consented to make provisions for this lady, for she would have been entitled to the position of marchioness if he had married her. Of course, said Sir Edward, it had been a considerable disappointment, and grief, to her, and a great break in her life. The Marquess had agreed to settle her the sum of £50,000, and give her an indemnity for all costs.

One newspaper recorded: 'A gasp of astonishment ran through the crowded court when the amount that Miss Markham was to receive was thus disclosed. At first people could scarcely credit it. Such a sum was the largest that had ever been granted by way of damages. It set up a record.'

When the hubbub in court had died down, Sir Edward added that he was glad that the case had thus terminated, and he hoped that it would lead to the happiness of both the plaintiff and defendant, and he certainly desired to say nothing against the Marquess.

Daisy in her becoming black satin, with her black and white

chiffron hat sat listening to the news of her great fortune with becoming modesty.

Mr. Duke (for the Marquess) then rose to admit that Sir Edward Carson was right in saying that there was no question as to the fact of a promise to marry. The only question was what compensation the defendant should pay to the plaintiff. Sir Edward had read the letter in which the mutual relationship between the parties was broken off, and it was impossible to hear it read without recognising that there was a very *sincere* attachment between the parties. At the time of the engagement the defendant was heir apparent to the marquisate of Northampton, and he had no expectation of any very early succession to the title. He felt bound to submit the proposed marriage to his father, who had laid on his son a most absolute prohibition and ultimately obtained from him, as it happened within a very short time of his untimely and lamented death, the most solemn engagement that he would not pursue the desire that he had to marry the plaintiff.

The impression left in the minds of the listeners was that it was a deathbed promise which had to be fulfilled, which was not, of course, strictly true, but it sounded dramatic in court.

The Marquess had no hesitation in agreeing that the sum mentioned was a reasonable provision to be made. Mr. Duke added, in that offhand way which people assume towards other people's money, it was not an ungenerous compensation – in so far as money *could* compensate for the plaintiff's disappointment.

Mr. Justice Bucknill agreed as to the Marquess's warm, deep and sincere affection for the plaintiff. As to the money, it was not for him to express any opinion about that, except that it was accepted by the plaintiff, and given in a generous spirit which dictated to the defendant that provision should be made for her – the sum had his fullest approval – as well it might.

After the court had been cleared, the Press crowded round a relative of Daisy's who happened to be accompanying her. 'This case,' said the lady, 'is lifted far above the ordinary breach of promise action. There is nothing sordid or mercenary about it, because a great romance lies behind it.' Miss Daisy said nothing.

But the rumours amongst the Marquess's relatives and friends were rife. May Fortescue, a soprano from the Savoy Operas had netted £5,000 for her broken heart – and that had been considered a vast sum. £50,000 – half a million in modern terms – seemed incredible. When the gasps of shock had died down in the higher social circles, when other young men who had been guilty of impetuosity or indiscretion were slowly recovering their equilibrium, and other young ladies had had their hopes groundlessly raised, tongues began to wag.

Miss Daisy was quite prepared to do a great deal of laundering of dirty linen in public. She was a woman cheated of great riches and position. She cared little what she said in open court if her allegations could bring some pecuniary advantage. It was one thing for a dashing young subaltern to stand his ground against a predatory lady but now the whole situation was changed. The Earl had become the Marquess, and he had his position, his family, and his responsibilities to consider. On the other hand the stakes for Miss Daisy were much higher – and she raised them. Following the advice of his Counsel the Marquess capitulated, and paid up.

It was also generally believed that this was not the first time that Miss Daisy had threatened gentlemen, and been compensated out of court for her broken heart.

There was a seven year gap in Miss Markham's stage career. In 1918 she appeared in *You Never Know, Y'Know*, and in 1920 blossomed out grandly into management. 'Daisy Markham's Season' at the St. James's Theatre presented *The Mystery of the Yellow Room* by Gaston Leroux, starring Sybil Thorndike and Nicholas Hannen. In 1922 she played Diana in *The Faithful Heart*, and in 1930 her last appearance was in a play called *Two to One*, less handsome odds than she received in her famous court case. She then seems to have disappeared into the wings of time with her comfortable settlement to console her.

The Marquess served with gallantry in the 1914 war, was wounded and awarded the D.S.O. and the Order of Leopold II of Belgium. When the war was over he made the suitable marriage to the bride his late father might have chosen for him, the Lady Emma Marjory Thynne, daughter of the 5th Marquess of Bath. The marriage took place in 1921 when the great slaughter was ended, and Lord Northampton felt he could settle down to administer his estates and father a family. But by this marriage, he had no children.

He remained, however, partial to the ladies, and especially to 'good lookers'. One of his relations said that he usually chose women who had all the appearance of 'handsome horses' racy and clean limbed.

It took a second world war to alter the shape of his life, and his family. At a time when many of the men on his estate had joined up, and were being replaced by the Women's Land Army, an army officer's daughter came to work for him. Eventually he married her when he was already fifty-seven. By this second wife he had two daughters born in 1943 and 1944, and then as a bonus for the signing of the second Peace in his lifetime, he, at long last, at the age of over sixty produced two sons born in 1946 and 1947. His inheritance was secured in the direct line.

The Marquess married for the third time at the age of seventy-three, but his wife died in 1972, and he lived on as a widower until the ripe old age of ninety-two.

His son, who inherited his titles and estates was in his thirties, the age that his grandchildren might have been had he married his dearest Daisy. Possibly when the old Marquess had looked back over the long span of his life, he could no longer remember being Daisy's despairing Bim, or of uttering that absurd sentiment 'If only I could escape from my position'. No doubt Daisy herself, settlement and all, had long since departed to that bourn where there are no settlements and no blackmail.

But Daisy had had her brief hour, and while it could not accurately be said that virtue had triumphed, it could be said that an expression of wide-eyed innocence can be used to secure a life of comfortable ease. Unlike the *Daily Telegraph*, Daisy had looked at the *'dessous des cartes'*, and played them to advantage.

CONNIE GILCHRIST, COUNTESS OF ORKNEY
or
From Tights to Tweeds

On 19 July 1892 Miss Constance Gilchrist was married at All Souls, Langham Place to the 7th Earl of Orkney. A contemporary gossip writer described the wedding with some embellishments.

> The approaching nuptials of the happy pair had been kept as secret as possible. None the less, the sacred edifice in which the ceremony took place was attended by more than a hundred well-wishers and the elite of the theatrical world. The bride was charmingly dressed in a dainty confection of grey silk, trimmed with green velvet and edged with Honiton lace. The noble Earl of Orkney was attired in an immaculate frock-coat, light trousers, and patent leather boots. On the conclusion of the service which was fully choral, the young couple and a band of friends enjoyed a recherche repast at the bride's house in Duchess Street, Mayfair.

It was the official end of Miss Gilchrist's theatrical career which had started at the age of twelve when she had danced at the Bedford Music Hall where the salary list included amongst the performers 'Gilchrist – twelve shillings', a payment of two shillings for each time Connie had danced.

With her wedding Miss Gilchrist drifted away from the gaze of the town which had once fêted her. When she married she had not acted regularly for some years. Occasionally she had appeared at a Charity concert and that was all. She was an enigmatic figure to her contemporaries and the gossip columnists of her time, and from the time of her retirement from the stage in her early twenties managed to steer clear of the scurrilous reports about her by merely ignoring them.

After her first appearance at the music hall in Camden Town, Connie Gilchrist was taken up by John Hollingshead, the owner of

the Gaiety Theatre, where he put on pantomimes and burlesques.*
'Practical John' Hollingshead flatly described his engaging Connie:

> Another music hall engagement that I shall always regard with satisfaction was that of Miss Connie Gilchrist. She was so young when I first made her a member of the Gaiety Company that we went through the form of an apprenticeship. She had appeared in a juvenile pantomime at the Adelphi Theatre and long before several friends, notably the late Montague Williams, advised me to engage her.

Her first appearance in pantomime was at Drury Lane in December of 1873 when she played the Prince of Mushrooms. The child performers, so much part of the Christmas scene, sang prettily:

> Oh take me on your knee
> And listen mother of mine,
> 'Twas the merry sound of the harp strings
> And their dancing feet so small
> A hundred fairies danced last night
> And the harpers they were nine,
> But oh the tales they had to tell
> Were merrier far than all.

The scene in which Miss Gilchrist danced was said to depict 'how the mushrooms spring up at the midnight hour'. Over the years it was not only mushrooms which sprang up to help Miss Gilchrist, it was a whole horde of stage door Johnnies.

But in the beginning of her career under John Hollingshead, it was her youth, her sweetness and above all her infantine innocence which appealed to the public. She was constantly photographed in every type of childishly fetching costume – muffs and tippets of fur, simple white dresses, stroking cats, looking appealing in snowstorms, or just looking innocently at the camera. The postcards which depicted her early career had much of the appeal of 'Bubbles' in the Pears' Soap advertisement. When she was dressed in the heavy evening dresses of a grown-up lady, with jewellery, she seemed as if she were wearing her mother's clothes.

Her attractions were her long slim legs and her shy violet eyes peeping out from her corn-coloured fringe. A picture of her as Shi-Ning (The Slave of the Lamp) in *Aladdin* shows her with her

* For an explanation of burlesque see p. 2.

little short tunic, her tiny conical Chinese hat, her fairy wand, and her innocent expression.

Hollingshead wrote: 'I did all I could to make her comfortable in the theatre, and she repaid me by quiet and amiable conduct and a determination to remain with me as long as I continued in management.' It is the picture of the amiable pupil anxious to learn. In 1878 when *Jack the Giant Killer* was the attraction for Christmas, Connie appeared in *Young Fra Diavolo*, a burlesque by H. J. Byron, and in this she 'was advanced to the front as a juvenile dancer, mastering the skipping-rope dance'.

The Skipping-Rope Dance was to bring her fame and fortune. Whistler saw her at the theatre, and painted her as *The Girl with the Skipping Rope*, a title he later changed to *The Girl in Gold*. Caught for ever in paint was the girl with her innocent expression, her heavy blonde fringe, her puzzled eyes, her long slim legs, and her tiny laced boots. The Victorians cherished the image of the innocent child, and Miss Gilchrist epitomised this. She was immediately nicknamed 'The Child', and her sayings and doings were chronicled in detail for the delectation and amusement of the town. For her speciality was singing a risqué song while opening her innocent eyes supposedly without understanding the import of the verses or the dialogue she was given. It was a tantalising combination which brought the young men flocking to the stage door to try to solve the enigma.

Miss Gilchrist's stage career stretched from *Goody Two Shoes* in 1876, *Jack the Giant Killer* in 1878, to *Pretty Miss Esmeralda* in the same year. But in 1879 with the painting of the girl with the skipping-rope she became part of the burlesque team at the Gaiety Theatre.

But not everyone was as enamoured of little Miss Gilchrist as the gentlemen who clustered round the stage door. An interview with an imaginary child star 'Baby Bangle', a caricature of Connie, has her lisping: 'I have been very kindly treated by audiences. They have shown their appreciation of my efforts by gifts of bouquets, rings, lockets and food – particularly the last of which I am exceptionally fond. Some people do say I'm like Miss Vaughan [Kate Vaughan was one of John Hollingshead's great stars of Gaiety burlesque], but I don't think this is fair.'

From 1879 to 1884 Connie played almost exclusively in burlesque – Lord Ladida in *Dick Whittington*, and *The Forty Thieves*, Robbiny Ray, Baron Montgiron in *The Corsican Brothers and Company*. This latter was a skit on Irving, who had to be placated by Hollingshead who presented him with the original stick which Tom King had used when he created the character of Sir Peter Teazle for Sheridan. 'The Child' invariably appeared in her short tunic and tights, in fact *Fun*, that rival to *Punch*, remarked that in one production 'Miss Gilchrist seemed depressed by the necessity of appearing in feminine apparel.'

In 1885, at the age of twenty-two, she retired. From then on she only appeared from time to time in charity performances. It was said that Miss Gilchrist was in the fortunate position of not being dependent upon her profession. 'She had a not inconsiderable private fortune.'

Connie Gilchrist: 'Audiences have treated me kindly with gifts of rings, lockets and food' (*The Bat*)

In April of that year *The Bat* recorded 'that dear little doll Connie Gilchrist, another of the Gaiety chucked divisions, gave a song and dance from the dead and dreary *Camaralzaman*'. This was one of the last shows in which Connie appeared for Hollingshead, and it had not been a success. On the first night *Fun* noted that the company showed a cheerful reliance on the services of the prompter. But *The Bat* was not criticising the piece but Miss Gilchrist herself, adding that when she was dancing, 'A lover in the pit threw a note to her but fearing that it might be dynamite I gallantly rescued it, but hereunder beg to proffer it to its rightful owner:

129

'Again a vision charmed our eyes
Of her who filled the place,
Of one whose mem'ry never dies,
And filled so well that her we prize
As pattern now of grace;
In skirt of saffron hue bedight
And hosen silk of mauve
She came and gave the same delight
That ever did the Child excite
As magic spells she wove.
We've mourned to see her seem so pale
But paled her power not,
Though form may look too fairly frail,
Be sure her charm will e'er prevail,
She'll never be forgot.'

The Bat was not pleased at Miss Gilchrist's retirement. They had promoted her and cherished her and publicised her, it was hardly her place to retire at the age of nearly twenty-three. At the end of 1885 James Davis writing as Pipistrel in *The Bat* addressed a long open letter to her which throws a somewhat different light on her private means.

29 December 1885.

My dear Constance,
    I did not intend to write to you at present, meaning to deny myself that pleasure until about the 23rd of next month when I would have accomplished a double purpose by congratulating you on your 23rd birthday and mentioning a few facts which I am sure will interest you. But for the last week or so, rumour, with its lying tongue, has been busy with your private affairs, and I feel it my duty as one of your oldest and loyalest friends to let you know what the world says and why the world says it. Not that rumour's falsehoods will affect you. Some young actresses rush off to their solicitors the moment an unfavourable report about them goes the rounds. They sob their dear little hearts out at antagonistic criticism and send their guardian mothers to threaten malingerers. You do not care twopence what people say of you, or what they write about you.

The Bat had reported some two months before that Miss Constance Gilchrist 'has at length found a suitable mate, and that she will within the next two months be led to the hymeneal altar by an interprising and popular young officer of the Brigade of Guards. My best wishes to the young couple.'

130

The Bat's best wishes were premature, Miss Gilchrist was not led to the altar. So Pipistrel had had his ear to the ground, and had come up with nothing to Miss Gilchrist's advantage. If people failed to appreciate Miss Gilchrist's charms, she appeared to be immune to jealous women or stupid men. If they sneered at her ways of proceeding, and misinterpreted her motives, her motto, wrote Pipistrel, was 'they may think what they like'.

By 1885, she had acquired a house in Duchess Street, Mayfair, where she lived quietly, entertaining friends to a feast of intellectual conversation. This did not deceive *The Bat*.

While cultivated cunning and elaborate reticence to disclose to the most inexperienced that which lies beneath them, there is often unfathomable mystery attaching to apparent frankness. That is what I might call the Gilchristian philosophy. For you have been before the public many years now, and they still wonder at you, and argue about you. Some are sure of one thing, others pooh pooh the very idea and ask if all the men – of whom they give such a precise catalogue – are imbeciles – or what? But the very fact that there still remains a doubt is a standing tribute to your originality for assuming that your friends are right, and your detractors are wrong; you have achieved a position which in fact no other actress has ever dared attempt before, a position which in fact would not be tolerated in any other civilised city in the world. For only in London are there actresses who, while communicating with the pitch of the profession, seek to remain themselves undefiled.

The Bat was understandably annoyed at this Mona Lisa from the burlesque stage. She had eluded all the strictures which journalists cast upon her. But the writer went on to list the advantages which had adhered to Miss Gilchrist's lucky skipping-rope.

Jewels and compliments have been showered on you by the smartest young men of the day. Nearly every noble family in the United Kingdom is represented on your visiting – I was going to write *subscription* list. A popular sporting journal was at one time entirely devoted to your eulogy. You have patronised every popular supper room in town, changing your cavalier as opportunity offered, and you have had every luxury your young heart has desired and they have been many.

Connie infuriated the writer. Her violet eyes remained as unclouded as ever – she had used no disguise. Her escorts fetched her boldly from the stage door. She supped with them, in public, à deux, and then was borne home in triumph by her cavalier, in triumph, or perhaps in hope, queried *The Bat*.

For *The Bat* was fairly certain that the Duke of Beaufort had bought her the house in Duchess Street, but did not name him. There was no doubt that she concealed nothing. Should she be given a diamond necklace by an admirer, *The Bat* noted, 'valued at goodness knows how many thousands', it had been proudly displayed to 'your envious sister artists and dilated on by them, their acquaintances, and all Clubland'.

> Now [wrote the Bat] that Viscount de Blue Point is the man in possession you preside at his little dinners, go about with him from morning till night, and everybody knows just exactly as much as you want them to know and not one iota more. If you had anything to conceal the doubt which has existed has been cleverly created; if there is nothing between you and your gentleman acquaintances but an honest friendship then you have been stupid. . . .

But there *The Bat* was quite wrong, and in the next sentence went on to contradict its own views.

> It is worth recalling that while boobies have been the acknowledged support of the theatre you have chosen for companions intellectual high bred gentlemen. Clever men have loved you. . . . No gentleman of property and position can be said to have finished his education until he has been abandoned by you.

But even her rejected suitors had some solace, admitted *The Bat*, for Miss Gilchrist surrounded herself with beautiful companions 'who look up to you, and admire you and while wondering how it is done, are grateful for the crumbs of mankind which fall dejected from the skirts of the most petted and profusely provided-for young lady of the stage'. The secret of Miss Gilchrist was forever to dance like a marsh light before the eyes of the writer on *The Bat*. How did she manage to be so open, and yet so reticent?

Pipistrel guessed that the old Duke of Beaufort, sixty if he was a day, had set Miss Gilchrist up in her admirable house in Mayfair. How was it that a girl who had started at twelve shillings a week, and even at the height of her fame could hardly have put away the thousands needed to lead the life of a grand lady of leisure, could keep her success so quiet? The open letter concluded by admitting, 'your power is permanent and no matter how angry a dismissed suitor may be, no matter what his anguish, his jealousy, his feelings of resentment – to love you once is to love you always.' It might be suspected that Pipistrel himself was one of those angry and frustrated suitors.

But *The Bat* continued to plug away at the Duke. In 1886 they announced the Duke's birthday on 1 February, adding a quotation from Jorrocks: 'Hunting is the sport of kings; the image of war without its guilt, and only five and twenty per cent of its danger.' Perhaps the writers on *The Bat* felt that Connie was a good huntress, and achieved her aims with only twenty-five per cent of the dangers which other women faced.

They had another glancing shot at the Duke a week later, and decided to interview him as a representative of the old school of gallants. The Duke was quite cheerful and open about his age, and his generation.

'The boys of today,' said the Duke, 'are every bit as good as they used to be. They lead pretty nearly the same lives as they used to when I was a youngster. It has always been the same. Turn to an old comedy of Farquhar or Wycherley, and with a very few alterations the habits of the young men described therein are very similar to those of today. Boys turned night into day, or day into night, just as the lads do now.'

When asked what the differences were between the forties of his youth, and the eighties of the present day, the thing which struck the Duke most forcibly was 'with regard to the ladies. One *never* used to see a young lady in Society till five o'clock in the afternoon. They had their drawing or music lessons, and worked thoroughly during the day. They were a great deal better informed than are the girls of today.'

The Duke's predilection for learned young ladies possibly explained why Miss Constance Gilchrist entertained only gentlemen of wit and culture.

What other changes had the Duke seen?

'Well, in the matter of tobacco. In my day if a boy in the Guards had been seen smoking in the streets he would have been sent for by his Commanding Officer.'

'The Thames took the place of the Park, didn't it?'

'Not in my time,' said the Duke, 'The steamers killed that. Before the steamers there used to be fours and eights kept in Chelsea Reach. My father used to belong to an eight.'

'And of an evening if the boys didn't dine at home, where would they go?'

'There were no restaurants in those days.' Then the Duke paused.

'Yes, there was Verreys, but no one thought of dining *there*. We used to go to The Thatched House Tavern, Hatchetts, or Limmers – that last was the principal place. Of course,' added the Duke, 'club life was only just beginning to be understood.'

What he meant by that cryptic remark remains as obscure as Miss Gilchrist's motives. Possibly that clubs afforded an excuse and a means of escape from wives and responsibilities.

The Bat interviewer wanted to know where everyone went after dinner.

'In the season there was the opera – everybody had his stall, or his share of an omnibus box, so that your friends knew where to find you.'

Asked about theatre the Duke was categorical. 'I don't think one went to theatres as one does now. They were,' he added grandly, 'an amusement entirely reserved for the middle classes.'

'What about music halls?'

'They were not the music halls which you know,' said the Duke. 'There was the Crown and Anchor in the Strand where there used to be masked balls, and then there was the Piccadilly Saloon where one used to meet a curious combination of Gentlemen and blackguards all hobnobbing together – until they naturally quarrelled.'

'London does not seem to have been overstocked with places of amusement.'

To this the Duke, remembering the heyday of his youth, could not agree.

'You forget – or you never knew – the Hells. All of us belonged to Crockfords. Those who didn't would play hazard at the Hells. Why, within a furlong of St. James's Street there must have been at least twelve or fourteen. There were four, I think, in St. James's Street itself, three in Albemarle Street, and five or six in Jermyn Street.'

'Possibly the boy of the period', said the representative of *The Bat* anxious to underline the generation gap, 'had more ample opportunity than the lad of today for going under?'

But again the Duke could not agree.

'Much of a muchness – if we had gambling hells, you have got very convenient suburban race meetings. When a boy comes to grief today he is despatched to Manitoba – or some such place. Then Boulogne used to receive him.'

The Duke could regard with equanimity the 'going under' of young men, if they played too deep they had only themselves to blame.

'Perhaps Society itself has altered?'

'Enormously,' said the Duke. 'It is much larger than it was.

134

Barriers have been broken down, and it is simply impossible for Society to be as exclusive as once it was.'

'What has done it?'

The Duke was in no doubt about that. 'Money,' he said simply. 'In the old days if one was asked to receive a lad or man of birth and breeding, one asked who he was, and expected the names of his father and mother as a guarantee that he would behave himself. Or he had been to one of the big public schools, or at either of the universities, or was in a crack regiment. Only gentlemen were supposed to go to public schools, or be allowed to join a smart regiment. Now if a man has got wealth – no matter how – he is received.'

'But do you think money entirely has done it?'

'Not entirely – there has been a levelling up, or a levelling down – a fusion of classes.'

'In your opinion has that been of good result?'

The Duke considered the question for a moment. 'Yes, certainly, I think it has! It has placed things on a broader bottom. People know people between, when in other days there would have been an impassable gulf. Personally I am very pleased, as the removal of the old barriers has enabled me to meet some very charming persons, and to form some very delightful friendships.'

Not a word was mentioned of Miss Connie Gilchrist who perhaps was disposed to entertain the Duke to uplifting conversation, now that she had the leisure to do so.

But the Duke and Miss Gilchrist had their detractors. The picture of *The Girl in Gold* gave rise to gossip which gathered momentum, even after her retirement.

On arriving from an artist's studio where she had been posing Miss Constance Gilchrist took to the burlesque stage. There she fascinated the golden youth of London by her habit of giving utterance to the most dangerous remarks with no apparent understanding of their real import. She had a pair of peculiarly liquid blue eyes that proved to be her fortune. At any rate they captured the Duke of Beaufort, who astonished London society by setting her up in a magnificent mansion in the heart of the West End; and for a season or two she was the subject of satire and envy in Rotten Row and other fashionable haunts.

Miss Gilchrist's liquid blue eyes gave nothing away. Neither the insinuation of *The Bat* nor the gossip of the clubs affected her, she kept her own counsel. She had been the subject of gossip for so many years, she could weather it without giving anything away. Even *The*

The 8th Duke of Beaufort. 'The removal of old barriers has placed things on a broader bottom'

Bat was forced to admit that she was as popular and sought after, and as much written about when she was not acting, as when she was. A judge professing judicial ignorance asked: 'Who is Connie Gilchrist?' – causing outbursts of hilarity in court at the very idea of anyone asking such a foolish question. Everyone knew about Connie Gilchrist. *The Bat* was annoyed that she continued popular.

> You enjoy [wrote that journal in its open letter] all the privileges of being the first London lady of the stage without necessary restrictions of doing anything definite. How long this state of things can last it would be impertinent of me to surmise. At present you are young and beautiful so that if the spirit moves you, you can send a devoted admirer of years to the rightabout in five minutes.

It was extremely irritating for the scandal sheets that they could find out nothing, and that Miss Gilchrist sailed on – comfortably placed, fêted, and immune to attacks.

136

The elderly Duke when asked by a Frenchman for an explanation of the letters K.G. after his name, smilingly replied that they stood for Konnie Gilchrist. Officially it was reported that the Duke was a great patron of the lighter side of the theatre. He was interested in Miss Gilchrist, and keenly aware that she needed help in her business affairs.

But the journalist in 1885 had not give up hope that Connie might return to the stage to delight them once more. On 29 September *The Bat* announced:

I learn from the Athenaeum that the Trustees of the Gilchrist Fund have arranged for a course of six lectures in five Lancashire towns during October and December. As I know of only one Gilchrist I would suggest the following subjects:
1) On skipping as a fine art
2) Infantine precocity as applied to burlesque
3) Medieval mashing as compared with that of the present day
4) On vacillation with special regard to the Stock Exchange
5) On the theory of resting
6) On self-preservation.

Numbers three and four of *The Bat*'s list were presumably as close as they could get to naming the Duke in connexion with Miss Gilchrist.

But still Miss Gilchrist vouchsafed no reply to these attacks. A month later she presided at a very successful Sunday dance for John Hollingshead. 'Miss Agnes Hewitt was generally voted the leading attraction of the entertainment – winning hands down from her – at one time – bosom friend Miss Connie Gilchrist.'

During the season Connie appeared in a box at Covent Garden to hear Madame Patti singing *La Traviata*. 'Prominent among the audience was Miss Connie Gilchrist whose high notes will no doubt have improved when next she honours the stage by appearing on it. I was pleased to see John Hollingshead with her – for such a combination shows the good fellowship existing between members of the dramatic profession albeit they are both out of work.' Madame Patti, said the critic, was in good voice, and seemed not in the least put out by the shoddiness of the dirty scenery, or the shabby cheap costumes. She was delighted to be with her London audience again, in spite of being weighed down with twelve baskets of flowers and a huge cushion of blossoms which she could hardly carry. Miss Gilchrist in her box was seen to clap her white gloved and genteel hands.

Apart from frequenting the opera, appearing occasionally in charitable performances, Miss Gilchrist attended many society functions.

'One of the smartest balls of the season was that given by Viscount Grey de Wilton, supper and wine both of the choicest from the Bristol Hotel. Two bands playing. His Lordship entrusted the distribution of invitations to Miss Connie Gilchrist, Mrs. Marini and Mr. Arthur Roberts, and the result must indeed have been flattering to the noble host. During the cotillion magnificent fans were presented to the ladies and dancing was kept up till six o'clock in the morning when breakfast was served.'

And then Miss Gilchrist's carriage was called and she swept off to her mansion in Mayfair.

The last appearance which she made on the stage was at the benefit performance of Nellie Farren who had been seriously ill. She was one of the best-loved and most outstanding stars under John Hollingshead, and a huge subscription list was set in train.

From tights ...

The Girl with the Skipping Rope
by Whistler

The General Committee was headed by the Duke of Beaufort, that kind patron of burlesque, and was under the special patronage of the Prince of Wales, another appreciator of tights and skipping-ropes. Amongst the long list of performers was Miss Connie – positively her last appearance on any stage. She played in *Nicholas Nickleby* as Tilda Price opposite Nellie Farren as Smike. The performance made over £7,000 – a considerable sum at the time.

For the next five years Miss Gilchrist lived quietly in her house in Duchess Street. She never appeared on the stage again. Both tunic and tights, and indeed skipping-rope, had been laid aside for ever. No doubt they had served their purpose.

138

Then in 1892 when she was nearly thirty, she was married to Edmond Walter Fitz-Maurice, who had succeeded to the title of Earl of Orkney after the death of his uncle three years earlier. The wedding was simple. A cousin of the bridegroom attended as best man, a niece of the bride was the only bridesmaid. The Duke of Beaufort, now nearly seventy, gave the bride away, and the two witnesses were the bride and bridegroom's respective solicitors.

to tweeds
The Earl and Countess of Orkney

This latter no doubt a prudent move on the part of the bride, and the Duke. The young couple then left for a honeymoon at Minehead.

It proved to be a long and happy marriage. The couple settled down at one or other of their country houses. The Countess was photographed wearing a high-necked dress, patting a large dog, and as the years wore on she merged into a background of tweed and dogs, and became indistinguishable from any other country-loving countess. Only the picture of the Gold Girl with her mauve stockings, her long spindly legs and her short tunic remained as a reminder of the golden days of the past.

The butterfly signature of Whistler recorded a butterfly who had become a tweedy chrysalis.

139

THE PLAYER PEER
or
Third Wife Lucky

In his autobiography, which was published in 1928, James Francis
Harry St. Clair-Erskine, 5th Earl of Rosslyn wrote:

'How many people have said to me: "What a fatal fascination
you have for women, Harry!"'

'And how often have I replied: "You mean what a fatal fascination women have for me!"'

He realised that he had been looked on as a rake and a roué, yet
wondered if his critics quite realised the sharp difference between
the artist and the degenerate. The 5th Earl of Rosslyn put himself
firmly into the category of the artistic. He had had his fortune told
many times and each time the same answer came up: 'You have a
great sense of the artistic – you admire beautiful things.' He admitted he did admire beautiful things, including women, and asked
himself the rhetorical question: 'Have I ever by admiration harmed
a woman in my life either cruelly or intentionally? Never!'

Lord Rosslyn was looking back over his long and extraordinary
life and pondering the shifts and turns of the roulette wheel, the
running capacity of various horses, and the strange quirks of various wives. Perhaps he should never have married. He felt perhaps
that flitting from flower to flower would have been a better idea
after all.

'I have loved solitude till it was succeeded by boredom. I have
loved companionship till the boredom of my mate has made solitude preferable. Give me the flowers of the country, the song of the
birds, the poetry of rippling streams, or the rush of turgid seas, give
me the sunshine ...'

To the outsider contemplating Harry's life, the thought springs
only too readily to mind that Harry had sunshine all the way.
Whatever happened to Harry was speedily remedied by some handy
millionaire, newspaper magnate, king, duke or even lady, only too
ready to help out in Harry's self-inflicted troubles. It is patently

obvious that he had charm in large quantities, charm which stood him in good stead throughout his long career of girls and gambling.

Harry was born in 1869. His mother was a widow with two daughters when she married the 4th Earl of Rosslyn in 1866. One of Harry's half-sisters was the notorious Daisy, Lady Brooke, mistress of Edward VII, and the other half-sister, Blanchie, became Lady Algernon Gordon-Lennox. Harry was the welcome heir to the earldom, and the first son of his mother, so he was born to great rejoicing and ringing of bells.

By many curious coincidences and the grapevine of Edwardian society, Harry was connected with some of the other characters in this book. His mother was a FitzRoy, of the Euston family, and therefore related by marriage to the notorious 'Flash Kate'. Blanchie had married into the same family as Marie Tempest. The Prince of Wales became godfather to one of Harry's children, and the Duke of Cambridge, husband of the charming Columbine, was always kind and helpful to him. Harry knew everyone and went everywhere, he was a mirror of Edwardian society, reflecting all its charms and many of its weaknesses.

After being born, the next thing that happened to Harry was that he was sent to prep school. The whole of his school and regimental life was peppered by nickname dropping. At prep school there was 'Grev' Verney, (afterwards Lord Willoughby de Broke), 'Pudding' Sudley (afterwards Lord Arran), 'Pickles' Lambton (brother of Lord Durham) and Johnny Moncreiffe known as 'The Fusee'. Passing on to Eton he met 'Slack' Brand (afterwards Lord Hampden) 'Punch' Philipson, and 'Fatty Lambert' (afterwards Lord Cavan).

The masters at Eton seem to have been more direct and intelligent than Harry. The headmaster asked him the leading question: 'Why don't you work harder, Loughborough?' Harry's dislike of work worried his father for the Earl was serious minded and alleged to be artistic. He wrote verse and was given to writing reproving letters to his family. Occasionally he found cause for pleasure. Writing from darling Daisy's house at Easton, near Dunmow in the spring of 1882 he was able to praise Harry:

My dearest Harry,
    I cannot tell you with what delight we received your telegram saying you were in Remove and it has proved to us not only that you had used the good abilities which God has given you satisfactorily and honestly but that when it came to the test of examination you were able to command your knowledge and apply it to the task imposed on you.

His father pointed out that his son was intelligent, but this has its disadvantages:

> to one so flighty and so quick as you are, the learning is there but the key is missing. You either open the wrong box or you fail to get at the right one.

A letter from m'Tutor at Eton, Arthur Ainger, proves that he had also carefully and sensibly summed the character of young Harry when he wrote to Harry's father:

> Flighty and self-indulgent he will continue to be till the years bring, if they ever do, discretion and something of genuine manliness. He disarms by his frankness and simplicity, it is as well to face the fact that he possesses a great capacity for making a fool of himself.... As to work he has taken it easy.

After leaving Eton, Harry went to Magdalen College, Oxford with two firm intentions – to hunt and play rackets. The following year he tired of Oxford and went to an army crammer's, and became a subaltern in the 'Blues'. Here he met more gentlemen with nicknames – 'Brock' (Lord Ranksborough) 'Squeezer' Combe, and 'Easy' Villiers.

The whole of fashionable Edwardian life opened out to him – there was his sister Daisy with her luxurious house at Easton; he was invited to Sandringham for the week-end. He began to play baccarat – bidding £600 for the bank although his allowance was only £240 a year. But this did not unduly worry him for his father had rather rashly promised to 'find' him in uniform, horses, and even to pay his debts. This latter turned out to be a far from sensible arrangement.

The easy luxurious living of the Edwardian age was beginning, or as Harry put it, 'Luxury was replacing Victorian Rep. My sister Brooke's at Easton was correctly fashionable – there was a desire to show, as becomingly as possible, one's silver and one's possessions.' Houses were filled with bright cretonnes, satin cushions, and silks, and vases with costly orchids, sweetly scented carnations and opulent roses. Equally opulent were the ladies who inhabited the drawing-rooms.

Harry was stationed as a junior subaltern at Windsor, and here he met and fell in love with Violet Vyner. His sister Daisy pointed out to him that apart from the fact that Violet was a pretty girl, she had other advantages, being, as Daisy put it, 'plentifully endowed'. Harry's parents were not at all in favour of this marriage. Like most parents they felt that Harry with his royal connections, his dash and his good looks could do much better than Violet Vyner, the daughter of a rich man with no title or advantages to her name. His response was to threaten in the classic fashion to go off to Africa. It is not quite clear what Harry was going to shoot in Africa, but he had bought himself a revolver, a sporting rifle, and a suit of thick khaki drill, and a map of South Africa. His parents were thoroughly alarmed. His father had been stricken with some form of paralysis and was very ill, and unwilling to let his son sail off to unknown dangers amongst natives and big game. He gave in.

Lawyers were sent for, and settlements were drawn up as a preliminary to a grand wedding. Not that these wedding preparations discouraged Harry from amusing himself with all the pleasures of the town, and meeting everyone worth knowing. The Duke of Beaufort introduced him to the beautiful Connie Gilchrist. The Duke (no chicken by 1890) was suffering from a bad attack of gout in his big toe, and asked Harry if he could take Connie dancing – which he obligingly did. It is always sensible to do a favour for a Duke. Harry was, at this time, the dashing romantic hero, both in his own eyes, and in the eyes of his fiancée. When he was staying at Ascot for the races, he used to climb over the wall of his fiancée's house for a few quick romantic words and kisses with her, and then climb back. His fellow officers (another clutch of nicknames – Buldoo Bryan, Di Rose and Ned Baird) took the ladder away and left him on the wrong side of the wall, necessitating a painful climb back.

Not that life in the army was all japes and joshing. It had its tough side. The unfortunate Harry developed shingles – he appealed to be exempted from a long route march. His request was turned down by his colonel. He enlisted the help of the head of the army, the royal Duke of Cambridge, who replied firmly that Harry must obey his colonel's orders. Shingles were no excuse for slacking.

Violet and Harry were married on 19 July 1890 at St. Michael's, Chester Square. It was a grand social occasion – amongst the bridesmaids was Lady Dudley, the first wife of the Lord Dudley who was afterwards to marry Gertie Millar. The Prince of Wales proposed the health of the happy couple. There were hundreds of guests and a thousand presents. Daisy, Lady Brooke, lent them the luxurious Easton Lodge for their honeymoon. As Harry wrote ruefully – if ever a marriage deserved to be a success, his first marriage did. Afterwards they journeyed to Scotland where the young couple were driven through the crowded streets of Kirkcaldy to Dysart House. It was, Harry remarked, a conqueror's welcome, with flowers all the way.

143

A few short weeks after the wedding Harry's father died, and he became Earl of Rosslyn at the age of twenty-one. Harry was very fond of his father and felt that if he had not died at the age of only fifty-five, he would certainly have been made Poet Laureate in the footsteps of Tennyson. From the poems of his father which Harry published in his book, it would seem an honour which the noble Earl might have achieved, but would not have been qualified to earn by merit.

Some time before he died the old Earl wrote to his wife: 'Sheltered from the wind in the spring sunshine scores of wild ducks are pluming themselves, playing in the exuberance of their seasonable desires on the clear waters of the lake.' This is exactly what Harry, his son, proceeded to do. Having come into his inheritance, he decided to enjoy life to the full. He trained and raced horses in England. The winter of 1891/1892 found him at his father-in-law's house le Château St. Anne at Cannes. It proved to be an unsuitable place for Harry. From there it was quite easy for him to travel to dear old Monte for two or three days a week. He gambled at Cannes and at Monte Carlo and after three months' stay while his wife was in delicate health, expecting her first child, he managed to lose £7,000. Undeterred by his loss he drew 50,000 francs out of the bank, went into the casino determined, as he put it, 'to have one last go before returning to England and sanity'.

He decided on trente et quarante – he saw that the black had won and put £480 on black. He had, like many gamblers, his theories on runs of luck. He believed in '*Suivez la couleur*'. He won on black fourteen times – he had recovered the whole of his three months' gambling losses.

'There was one more coup of apparently eight or nine cards, and I did not think these were sufficient for another shot. I began to *ramasser* my huge pile ... when I heard the players say "*Lâche, Poltron!*"'

Egged on by these nasty remarks he thought of trying again, but then saw red come up. It was an omen. He decided to go home. Friends of Harry had heard two dubious looking men saying: '*Là il s'en va*' and so the three Englishmen rushed off to get to the bank before it closed to put the money out of harm's way. Harry then bought himself a revolver, and was escorted to the station, allegedly pursued by *louche* characters about to snatch his happy winnings.

Once in England he went on to racing and backing horses and entertaining the Prince of Wales. 1892 was a high point – he won twenty-eight races with fifteen horses.

Although he and his wife were supposedly settled down at Dysart House, Harry seems to have spent most of his time travelling backwards and forwards to London, playing cards heavily at the Turf Club – any game of cards suited him – bridge, bezique – but chiefly piquet. He had a very good system for living his double life. He left home at ten o'clock at night, spent the night in the train and was in his bath in London at 8.00 a.m. On the return journey he reversed the process and took his bath at home. Apart from cards, horses and roulette, Harry was also a dedicated shot. He noted that in 1892 his game book showed that he had helped to kill 10,000 pheasants, and 3,000 partridges, and at Houghton, when one of eight guns, they had got 1,600 brace in one day.

Harry was forced to admit, looking back on this halcyon time, that he had squandered a great deal of money, but he had 'found time for formal duties at home'. The Duke of Cambridge, for whom he had a great respect, was doing one of his annual tours of inspection and he was staying with the Rosslyns when their son Francis was born on 16 November 1892. The gentlemen were celebrating the event (no doubt with copious libations of port) when Bertie Vane-Tempest kept on interrupting the Duke, and he had to be chased into the scullery to prevent the old Duke bursting out laughing. It puts the 'Head of the Army', as the Duke used to call himself, in a different and more genial light. Apart from his other pursuits Harry was excessively fond of billiards – and at Newmarket managed by one game of billiards to recoup the £3,000 he had lost on the horses.

He was beginning to borrow from money-lenders, and in the usual way of borrowers described them as 'scum'. Nor was his marriage going well, which was not surprising. Gentlemen who can only do a quick about-turn at home to have a bath in Scotland before leaving swiftly for the Turf Club in London, should not be surprised if wives take a less lenient view of their activities than they do themselves. 'Jolly good fellows' are seldom jolly at home. Nor were the drinking habits of the day conducive to a life of even-tempered happiness. Harry's lavish views on drink, written when he was fifty-eight, reflect a temperament which was easy going. 'When I was twenty-one I should think I "held" a quart of champagne and a quart of port. After my twenties, I was a port man – two bottles a day.' The result of all this good fellowship, was that he was sent for by his father-in-law Mr. Vyner. Vyner was quite blunt. Was it, he asked, true that Harry was making a fool of himself with one of the most beautiful women of the day? Harry had to admit that he had been attracted to her, but after all why not? He had known her since childhood. Mr. Vyner did not see why this fact meant giving the lady in question a tiara of diamonds and turquoise which cost over £2,000. From the facts which he wrote later when he was acting with her, *la dame au diadème* would appear to have been Lillie Langtry. Mr. Vyner also came up with the unwelcome news that the lady had not cherished this sentimental gift, but had sold it for half the price. His daughter Violet was suffering because of Harry's neglect. She was left for weeks on end with her children in a large house in Scotland with no husband.

Harry decided to reform and went back to Dysart. For a time all settled down, but when the races came round again, Harry was, like the runners, off. He went to Doncaster Races. There he met a bookmaker called Fry.

'Hello, my lord; I didn't expect to see you here. I've just had a telegram from Dysart.'

He showed Rosslyn the telegram. 'Put £25 on such and such a horse.'

The telegram was signed by an admirer of Lady Rosslyn who had come to take the errant husband's place in his absence. While the cat was away the mouse had begun to lick the cream.

By 1893 Harry was in debt to the tune of £125,000. 'For the first time in my life I was alarmed.' It must be noted that Lord Rosslyn did not seem to get alarmed very easily. But this time things had caught up with him, and he was forced to sell his race horses, his stud and Dysart House. He raised another mortgage for £107,000. He still remained quite optimistic about his life and to keep himself 'out of mischief', as he put it, took up Freemasonry very keenly and joined a number of different lodges. He seemed to feel that Freemasonry was some kind of therapeutic regeneration. His wife by this time had left him, and was living apart in a house provided by her father. She had refused to give up the gentleman who had placed the bet of £25 on the runner at Doncaster Races.

By 1897, the inevitable had happened – Harry was made bankrupt. At first he had hoped that his father-in-law Vyner would help him out, but, not surprisingly, Vyner felt that the best thing for Harry would be to be bankrupt. There was nothing like bankruptcy for restricting credit.

Here the Duke of Cambridge joined in, and when he heard that Harry was 'going smash', he offered £8,000 to help with the outstanding debts. Vyner pleaded with the Duke not to give the money. He wanted Harry to go bankrupt. Reluctantly the Duke had to comply with the family's wishes.

So on a sunny autumn morning Harry walked with his solicitor to the Bankruptcy Court. He was only allowed to keep the watch his mother had given him for his twenty-first birthday – cuff-links and studs had to go. To the last minute he had hoped that his relations would rescue him. 'They, however', wrote Harry bitterly, 'did not

146

share this view.' But the Duke of Sutherland, husband of his sister Millie, gave him a room in Stafford House and £400 a year.

Yet Harry, as always, was to fall on his feet. For some time past he had been a star of the amateur theatrical performances which had enlivened Edwardian country house parties. From the beginning he had always taken up acting with the greatest interest and zest, as he had done everything else from losing his money, his house or his wife.

The first part he had played was George D'Alroy in Tom Robertson's *Caste* at West Dean near Chichester, and then the gentry had given another two gracious performances at The Corn Exchange, Chichester to raise money for the local hospital. His approach to 'theatre' was off-hand. 'It never entered my head that *Caste* had been one of Robertson's chefs-d'oeuvre' – Harry did not know that the piece had been played by outstanding actors of the Victorian stage. The only thought in his head was how he himself was going to portray the character. Bitten by the bug of acting, Rosslyn began to get together amateur productions. He 'got up' *Diplomacy* in aid of Scottish charities with Elinor Glyn playing Dora. Other plays followed including *The Ladies' Battle* from *La Bataille de Dames*. There were the usual jealousies about casting. Miss Wilson (a guest with some acting ability) was cast in the small role of *ingénue*, while Lady Mar and Kellie played the leading part of the Comtesse. Harry thought this was absolutely correct. Lady Mar must play the important role – she was the hostess. Acting ability had nothing to do with social precedence.

It was perhaps natural when Harry went bankrupt that he should think of acting as an easy way to earn a living and retrieve his fortunes. Having left the bankruptcy court, he was standing outside a teashop in Mount Street when Seymour Fortescue A.D.C. to King Edward VII greeted him. He was immediately swept off to luncheon at the Café Royal – ate one of the best luncheons he ever remembered, washed down with claret – and discussed his plans for conquering the stage.

Fortescue noted that Harry was serious about going on the stage. It seemed a reasonable idea, and he took the man of the world view that 'it was not likely to be misunderstood by Harry's friends'. Armed by this official approval from the higher echelons, Harry dropped in to see Sir George Alexander at the St. James's Theatre. Alexander was uncompromising and said that Harry would hate the life, but if he was serious a chance had come up. Pinero was looking for a '*jeune premier*' for a new play he was putting on which was just going into rehearsal, and Harry was given a letter to Dion Boucicault who was casting the play, *Trelawny of the Wells*, and

Harry was given the part of Arthur Gower. He signed a contract in the autumn of 1897 – seven performances a week for £20.

A week later he was sitting on the stage hearing Pinero read the play. Harry had fallen on his feet again. The rehearsals lasted two weeks, which Harry thought too long. Being a 'quick study' he felt that a week's dress rehearsal would be a much better way of going about things. If there was one thing Harry did not lack, it was confidence. Although even he did have his diffident moments backstage.

He asked Irene Vanbrugh quite shyly – 'Do I really kiss you?'

Irene replied briskly, 'That depends on yourself.'

There were aspects of theatre life which seemed to have compensations.

To re-read the original criticism of *Trelawny of the Wells* is a curious experience. To a modern audience the pork-pie hats, the elastic-sided boots, the white stockings and above all the swish of the silken crinolines is an essential part of the charm of the piece. To the critics of 1898 they were an affront. The crinolines were dubbed grotesque, and preposterous. Other disadvantages were pointed out. 'The conscientiousness which guided the choice of undergarments displayed in the movements of the crinoline was deplorable from an aesthetic point of view.' Another critic wrote: 'Oh those crinolines! They seemed to dominate every act with their hideous hoops.'

Mr. James Erskine (reported to be the Earl of Rosslyn) had equally mixed notices. 'Mr. James Erskine has a great deal yet to learn before he can make us understand Rose Trelawny's devotion to Arthur Gower.'

'Mr. James Erskine, making his debut as the judge's grandson, scarcely justified his choice of the stage as a profession.'

Although one critic did admit that Mr. Erskine 'bore himself with sincerity', while *The Sketch* recorded, 'Mr. James Erskine, who is in everyday life the Earl of Rosslyn, plays the small part of Arthur Gower very cleverly indeed. It is rather curious by the way that his sister should also be a Gower – a Leveson-Gower.'

Miss Vanbrugh was more complimentary about Harry:

For the part of Arthur Gower, the management had rashly, but (as it turned out) fortunately, decided to engage Lord Rosslyn, who, taking the name of James Erskine, was making his debut on the professional stage – at that time rather an event for a member of the peerage. He was excellent. I have played with many Arthur Gowers since but the character has never been so well portrayed. He was to the manner born in the clothes of the period and his

148

natural breeding enabled him to strike just the right note in his association with the bohemian circle with which, in the play he found himself.

The pictures of Harry, playing hero to Irene Vanbrugh's heroine, show him wearing his clothes admirably, while the caricaturists when picturing the play emphasised his unaristocratic snub nose.

Lord Rosslyn as Arthur Gower with Irene Vanbrugh.
'He was to the manner born'

The play ran for 150 nights. This aspect of theatre bored Harry. There was nothing so tedious as repeating the same lines every night, added to which he had the chore of putting on and taking off his make-up. The only thing which he enjoyed was driving home with Irene and her 'dear old dresser' to have supper with Violet Vanbrugh and Arthur Bourchier.

From *Trelawny of the Wells* he went on to play Captain Rivers in Captain R. Marshall's *His Excellency The Governor*. It was a small part but obviously type-cast. He played an eager officer dashing back to warn the Governor of a native uprising. He rushed in covered with blood, to collapse on the drawing-room carpet. 'What

149

happened?' 'I didn't see the gates were closed, I galloped full against them.' This line, Harry noted with satisfaction, used to bring the house down.

Now that Harry was bankrupt he had no club to go to and found the time, when he was not acting, hanging very heavily on his hands. What to do? He decided to start a newspaper. Two of his friends were Alfred and Harold Harmsworth (afterwards Lords Northcliffe and Rothermere). They lent him the money to start a paper called *Scottish Life*. By 1898 he had been 'adjudicated' and so presumably was able to start an enterprise of this kind. He ran the paper almost entirely alone. He canvassed for advertisements, wrote half the articles and edited the rest, including the serial. He felt he was doing his best to retrieve the past. 'Without occupation we are dead, pawns in the great drama of life with no special reason for encumbering the earth', he wrote grandiloquently. Having effectively dished his fortune and his prospects, he felt disposed to draw trite philosophical conclusions from the débâcle.

In 1899 he was acting in *A Royal Family* wearing one of the most gorgeous uniforms he had ever seen. Like so many of Harry's

The Earl of Rosslyn as James Erskine.
'One of the most gorgeous uniforms I have ever seen'

enterprises the stage had begun to pall. The Boer War had broken out and he was for putting on a less exciting uniform and being off to the wars. The Fife Light Horse would not have him – his bankruptcy and the general raffish nature of his activities made him temporarily less than an officer and a gentleman. Just at the right moment the *Daily Mail* telegraphed him to go out and manage the 'Absent Minded Beggar Fund', a charity started by Maud Tree to help the soldiers. Alfred Harmsworth took him on as a war correspondent, giving Harry some pointers: 'I don't want dull, wishy-washy stuff; do something different from others, dashing and maybe dangerous. I am only giving you ten pounds a week, but you can get more from the *Daily Mail* on the spot. I'll keep your letters for you to make a book of. I've got you a camera from *The Sphere*, a new illustrated magazine which is just starting. Go and see about kit, which I shall pay for.'

So off went Harry to the wars where he became at once a roving correspondent for the *Daily Mail* and *The Sphere*. He began by reciting *The Absent Minded Beggar*, collecting money, and lunching out with various society ladies who awaited the return of 'their lords'. At Rondebosch he visited a hospital being run by Lady Henry Bentinck. Lady Henry, according to Harry, was a dream of beauty in a brown holland dress, a soft white fichu round her neck, a pretty straw hat with a pale blue ribbon to match a belt of the same colour and a dainty pinafore with a Red Cross armlet. She was, wrote Harry romantically, one of the angels of mercy who had given up the comforts of home to take her share in helping the wounded. She and her helpers seem to have pottered around handing out cigarettes to the troops while looking lovely.

Eventually he became tired of the social round and the recitations and the ministering angels. He decided to rejoin the army. Again he had difficulties but finally was allowed to join Thorneycroft's Mounted Infantry. General Buller sent a telegram: 'Rosslyn may proceed to the front on condition he does not correspond with any paper.' Journalists were no gentlemen and fighting could not be mixed up with reporting.

For three weeks Harry was able to fight and ride with Thorneycroft's. He admitted that he didn't like war, but he felt it was good for any young man to rough it. He only wanted to be with Thorneycroft's to see the fun. He fought at the battle of Pieters Hill and marched to the relief of Ladysmith. But then, having decided to resume his capacity of war correspondent, he set off with two guides to cross the Drakensberg Mountains and catch up with another part of the war. It took him nearly a week to get to Maseru – here he found Sir Godfrey Lagden who entertained him at the

Residency. He was amazed at Harry's feat of crossing Basutoland, but Harry's only comment was that it had been monotonous, and he would have found it much more enjoyable had he had a friend with him. He could have been talking of a little rough shooting in Norfolk.

After a couple of days' rest Harry determined to cross the Boer lines. Sir Godfrey, an old Africa hand who had been in the country sixteen years, advised against the feat. 'You want to go as near the precipice as possible without falling over it. I quite understand your ardour, but you should rest satisfied with your feat of having crossed Basutoland. I will help you as far as I can, but I cannot allow you to return here if you find you are unable to get through.' Sir Godfrey had preserved Basutoland as neutral in the war and he was not risking Harry being caught as a spy and having to take the blame.

Undeterred Harry set off and, after riding seventy miles in thirty hours, rode into a village thinking it was occupied by the British when it was in the hands of the Boers. 'A rough bearded man of an inferior class pulled me off my pony.' He was most indignant at being ordered into a cart seated for four but which already held *five* people. His pony was taken with its holsters and rug, and all he was left with was his camera, his waterbottle and a few shillings. One man jumped on the pony. Harry was indignant: 'My pony can't go another yard! It has already done about seventy miles during the last thirty hours, and I want food. I have had none since the previous night. I am starving.'

Harry glared at the Boers indignantly 'Surely you can behave like gentlemen.'

Loud laughs greeted this remark. After a few days he escaped from the Boer irregulars and made his way once more towards the British lines. He had not gone very far when he found himself in the middle of a battle – being fired on by both sides. He managed with difficulty to join the British side, but his luck did not hold. The British were attacked by a Boer commando, totally surrounded, and after a sharp battle against an enemy they could not see – they were forced to surrender.

Harry was not a good subject for imprisonment. 'It is sixteen days since I last touched upon my daily life.' He wrote in his diary that it was not the feeling of degradation which oppressed the imprisoned, but monotony, monotony, monotony! But he had overcome this quite simply – he had started another magazine. Written in Harry's own handwriting it was produced on 12 May, the 'hectographs' duplicating sixty-two complete copies of forty-eight pages each. The magazine was called *The Gram* because any piece of news received by the prisoners was called a gram. It was the kind of amateur production written to amuse any enclosed society full of local jokes (Lt. St....s gave a marvellous imitation of an elephant i.e. he was snoring), and jolly verses:

> Darling Jane,
> My wound is slight, do not be anxious dear.
> I'll soon recover, sweetheart, have no fear.
> It's a pity, Janey, that there's not
> The *slightest* chance of hubby getting shot.
> But he is just as safe down there at Durban
> As City clerk in English town suburban.
>
> List to the moral
> Better the censor's desk than warrior's laurel.

Less than a month later, the prisoners were liberated. In his character of war correspondent Harry immediately dashed down to the post office and sent off a cable announcing the news. He was standing on the balcony of the telegraph office when he heard a shout, 'Hello, there's Harry!' The Duke of Marlborough was greeting him back into civilisation.

From prisoner Harry resumed the role of player, starting at the top (as usual). He acted for Mrs. Patrick Campbell, for Herbert Tree at His Majesty's in a play which flopped, and in a tour of *The Queen's Necklace* playing Count Fersen to Mrs. Langtry's Marie Antoinette. This latter assignment had its compensations, for these two amateurs rehearsed while bobbing up and down in the sea opposite Lillie's cottage in Jersey.

By 1905 Harry's career seems to have begun to flag a little, and he went off to dear old Monte Carlo to cheer himself up. Here he met and fell in love with Anna Robinson.

Anna Robinson was an American actress who had been discovered by the impresario Charles Frohman and brought to England especially to take American parts. American heiresses were much in the news, and it was in this part that she appeared in *The Undercurrent* with A. E. Matthews, Violet Vanbrugh and Arthur Bourchier. 'The American girl (heiress to millions of dollars) was played spiritedly by Miss Anna Robinson. ...' said one critic. Another, although reluctantly admitting her attractions, had reservations: 'Miss Anna Robinson is so fresh and attractive that she always brightens the busy scene. She is handsome in all respects – save the fashion of her speech, her pile of dollars, however big, could not compensate for her Yankee intonation.'

Anna Robinson with A. E. Matthews

So Harry, now divorced, on his annual cheering-up visit to Monte met the lively Anna. From the *sous-entendu* of his gentlemanly account of the proceedings it would seem that she had a male escort: 'A charming companion, whose name I think it best to omit from the story.' Inspired no doubt by libations of champagne in a 'spirit of revelry' Harry and Anna carried out a form of old Scottish marriage 'on the telephone directory', there were two witnesses; Anna's gentleman friend, and the inevitable dear old concierge called Baptiste.

The following day Harry found that Anna had taken the whole thing seriously. Inspired by her beauty, and her newspaper cuttings which she prudently happened to have with her, Harry conceived the idea that they could become a handsome leading couple on the West End Stage. He asked her to marry him. She assured him she had enough money for their needs and a house in London. In his impetuous way Harry sent one of his usual telegrams – this time to a clergyman with easy-going views who would marry them. He was, wrote Harry, open minded on the subject of an innocently divorced man. The marriage was arranged, and they left for London. Harry's sister, Millie, the Duchess of Sutherland, made a last minute attempt to stop the marriage – it was useless. Forty-eight hours later Anna Robinson had become the Countess of Rosslyn. After the wedding there was a small lunch party – it consisted of the 'friend' who had kindly handed Anna over to Harry, the broad-minded vicar, and Anna's solicitor. As soon as the guests had left, Anna, to the consternation of her new husband, fell senseless to the floor.

Harry sent for her doctor. The doctor looked at the prostrate lady – he knew her well. He looked at Harry, his comment was terse. 'I suppose you know you have married a dipsomaniac?'

Neither Harry nor Anna could get work on the stage in the following miserable year. Harry's reaction to his troubles was to hire a yacht and go off on a holiday, and after running on a sandbank he managed to get to port at Trouville.

Harry's account of the events which followed (in breezy Trouville) differs somewhat from that of his wife. His story was that he met a charming lady Mrs. S. (decorously accompanied by her brother and a cousin). He asked them to dine. He went back to his yacht after dinner, and was contemplating a peaceful scene, when Anna came in late from the casino and caught him two violent hooks across the face. He realised she was drunk and tried to hold her down, but she screamed so loudly that people came running from neighbouring ships. Finally with a superhuman effort he managed to get her down to her cabin. The next day she said she had had enough of him – he could do what he liked with his yacht, and she left for that American Mecca – Paris.

The story which was told before Lord Mackenzie in January of 1907 differed in some small respects from Harry's. Lady Rosslyn (known in Scotland as the pursuer) brought the action for divorce. Lord Rosslyn was presently residing at 8 Rue Picot, Bois de Boulogne, Paris. He did not appear, and he made no defence. But Lady Rosslyn identified him from a photograph. Her story of the marriage was that they had settled down happily in her house at Norfolk Street, Park Lane. There had been differences between them but they had been patched up. In July of 1906 she went with her husband on a yachting cruise. On 17 August at Trouville her husband brought a lady on board the yacht, he introduced her as Mrs. Saunders. 'The pursuer had not known the lady before, and was somewhat surprised at the demeanour of Lord Rosslyn and this lady. Subsequently he took the lady ashore and did not return until half past eight the next morning – still in his dress suit. The pursuer asked him for an explanation – he did not give one, and she immediately left the yacht accompanied by her sister, and her maid. She had not lived with Lord Rosslyn since that date.' Evidence was then given that Lord Rosslyn and Mrs. Saunders had lived together at 8 Rue Picot, Paris, and as far as was known were still living there.

The decree was granted. There were always two sides to every divorce.

Harry was now jobless, wifeless, but once again happily footloose. He went off to South America, staying on various haciendas with rich South American landowners. By 1908 he was back in England. He had no home, and no money. His brother FitzRoy came to his rescue, and lent him a cottage near Maidenhead. It was a sweet cottage with a garden filled with old-fashioned flowers. There amongst the flowers he met Vera. He took one look at her – and fell in love with her.

She took one look at him, went indoors, sat down at the piano, and sang, for some reason which is not explained by Harry, Tosti's 'Goodbye'. Whether as a result of falling in love with Harry, or the menu, she could eat no supper, and he was obliged to feed her like some sick little bird with spoonfuls from his plate. The following day – after she had left – he opened his blotter and found a scribbled note. Vera had written: 'You are the dearest man in the world.'

He was shattered. Here was a lovely girl – his chance to build up a new life, but he was unworthy. All his life had been a 'misspent gamble'. How could he, a ruined roué, risk the happiness of a girl just twenty-one?

Vera, called 'Tommy' by her friends, was scooped up by her sister-in-law and immediately taken abroad away from the obvious dangers of getting mixed up with Harry. But he was in hot pursuit and followed her to Germany, stopping on the way only to have a quick gamble, and lose some money at Ostend. Eventually he caught up with 'Tommy' and her sister-in-law at Wiesbaden. The edict was final. There was absolutely no question of marriage for Vera, and certainly not marriage with Harry. His new-found love was hurried off to Langen Schwalbach. The bird had flown and he had no money to pursue. He heard a rumour that Alfred Harmsworth was staying in the neighbourhood. He took a gamble and hired an expensive car, driving the fifty miles to where Harmsworth was staying. Romantically inclined, and perhaps inspired by the news value of the romance of earl and girl, he immediately lent Harry some money to carry on the chase. So off he went to Langen Schwalbach. The girl was still there. Like the ending of some novel of 1900, Harry found her in another flower-filled garden and there, with the moonlight shining on her young face, she promised to be his wife.

He took the first train and boat back to England, and went straight to see his senior trustee (dear old Cullimore), who was delighted at the idea of Harry marrying and settling down. Harry arranged for a honeymoon, a house, and a bit more money from the estate. Having satisfactorily settled the practical details he hurried down to Dover to take the girl in his arms.

But his troubles were not entirely over. His future wife's solicitor Mr. Humbert had taken umbrage at the marriage, and refused to have anything to do with it. Captain George Bayley (Tommy's brother) confronted Harry and said that on no account could Harry marry his sister. Harry was very annoyed at his attitude, particularly as he was staying at the Ritz at the time and suffering from a sharp attack of lumbago. It was hardly gentlemanly to confront a man with lumbago in this way. But after a short chat, and the exercise of Harry's charm, the Captain calmed down.

On 8 October 1908 Vera (Tommy) was married to her Harry. From her photograph, taken at the time of her marriage, Vera was a good-looking girl with large dark eyes, soft dark hair and a slim figure. The mouth shows resolution which no doubt she needed. Harry's friends called her 'the Lion Tamer'.

Harry was nearly forty to Tommy's twenty-one. To some women the reforming of a rake is a challenge.

There is no moral to the tale of Harry – except that charm – and knowing the right people – can get a man out of the tightest spots.

GERTIE MILLAR
or
Always a bridesmaid, twice a bride

When Coward wrote, 'extraordinary how potent cheap music is' he was writing from the heart, a heart which remembered the past, and which remembered the London of the past, the theatre of the past, and above all the actresses of the past. Of all the actresses who symbolised the tunes and the charm of the world before the débâcle of 1914, Gertie Millar was the girl who lingered in the minds of the men who had lived at that time.

To later generations she was the Countess of Dudley, and journalists, in order to jog the memories of their older readers, would put Gertie Millar in brackets after her name. But Coward, remembering Gertie, was able in a few words to conjure up the feelings she evoked. 'To me when I was a little boy, and when I was a young man, she signified the essence of enchantment in the theatre. No one that I have seen or admired since had a quarter of her charm, or was in any way comparable to her.'

At the age of nine Noël used to save his pocket money and go once a week to see her in *The Quaker Girl* at the Adelphi Theatre. 'She possessed a magic that has remained clear in my memory all my life. I can see her now, dancing in the blue light of the *Pré Catalan* in Act III, dancing so lightly that she seemed barely to touch the stage, and singing in that light little voice: "Tony from America". In those early years I spent many hours waiting outside the stage door to see her come out, and get into her car. Once indeed she became aware of my persistent worship and gave me some flowers from her bouquet, which for years I kept reverently pressed in a bound volume of the *Play Pictorial*.'

When Gertie Millar had been on the stage more than ten years she wrote a simple little piece which brings to life the beginning of her career. She was the daughter of a Bradford mill-worker, and yet even to a 'hand' in a factory the stage was not considered to be either respectable, or suitable as employment for a daughter.

158

'My First Appearance' by Gertie Millar appeared in *The Sketch* in 1910.

I belong to the great army of child actors. I was not more than ten years old when I made my first appearance on the stage. Most children who go on to the stage do so, not merely with the consent of their parents, but in accordance with their deliberate desire. In that I was an exception to the rule. My parents had no idea of my being an actress, and were opposed to it. I had to talk my mother in to allowing me to act.

I lived in Bradford at the time, and whenever I could get my mother, or a friend, to take me to the theatre – I went. In those days the kitchen table was my stage, and on it I used to do my dances and sing the songs which I had seen, or heard, the real actors and actresses perform. My mother was always my interested audience of one, and I can recall her sitting and watching my sister and me play the Wolf and Little Red Riding Hood in scenes from the local pantomime.

One day I heard there was going to be a pantomime in which the children of the town were to take part. Without saying a word to anyone at home, except my sister, I went off to the manager, and was engaged. How I managed to attend all the rehearsals without my people being aware of what I was doing I can't tell. I only know I did it – until the day of the dress rehearsal, then I had to be in the theatre until midnight. I had to tell them.

The result was that she was sent to bed instead of going to the theatre. 'I howled.'

As a result of the howling, Gertie's sister took a hand in her career. It would not be fair for Gertie to miss the dress rehearsal. 'It was bound to cause inconvenience to other people.' The fact that Gertie would have been reneging on her contract with the panto-mime manager was the point which told in a working-class family, where time-keeping, and general respectability, and giving value for money reigned supreme. Gertie had said she would appear and she must not go back on her word.

The mother relented and Gertie successfully carried out her first engagement.

That little local engagement [wrote Gertie] was like the taste of blood to a tiger. I was dancing from morning till night, and I was singing when I was not dancing. The theatre was everything to me. Those were the days when the hallmark of the stage was golden hair, and every actress wore it either as a gift of heaven, or

159

through the genius of the peroxide bottle. If I saw a woman in the street with golden hair, I always followed her – in the hope that she might notice me, and I could ask her to get me into a theatre company, and I was always writing to managers to the same effect.

No one took any notice of her, or her letters. But Gertie was always persevering, she was not a Yorkshire lass for nothing. She heard that a man in the town was engaging a company for a concert tour – a shining week at the Town Hall, Pudsey. A friend – or her sister – managed to talk the manager round and persuaded him to come to Gertie's house, so that she could sing to him and achieve the height of her ambition – a whole week of singing and dancing on a real stage. She was taken on, and the week spread into several weeks, and from that engagement she heard of a pantomime which was being cast. That was just the very thing. Pantomimes were big business in the provinces before 1914. In pantomime a girl could make her name.

So Gertie Millar made her first appearance on the professional stage as the girl Babe in *The Babes in the Wood* at the St. James's Theatre, Manchester.

Remembering her debut, Gertie wrote:

> When I think of the preparation which a musical play involves, it is a little less than wonderful to me that I was allowed to play without having studied my part properly. I had a song in the pantomime, and I knew that thoroughly, but I never had a smattering of the words I had to speak. Still such is the inconsequence of childhood that I did not trouble in the least. I said whatever came into my head at the time, and gagged my part during the run – as if I were an experienced low comedian.

In a few sentences Gertie Millar managed to convey two things – her great confidence in herself, and her great simplicity. She knew that the stage was the place for her, and she knew that the public would love her. It was later admitted that her singing voice was 'hardly worthy of mention', and she had little dramatic ability. But she was enchantingly pretty and full of personality. Her every movement was filled with grace and sweetness. Grace and sweetness – those were the two qualities which the world in the days of *la douceur de vivre* demanded, and the manager of St. James's Theatre, Manchester was the first man to discover these shining qualities in Gertie.

In spite of her delicacy and grace, she was tough. People who saw her said she had some of the homespun qualities of Gracie Fields. Writing of her first appearance in pantomime, Gertie remembered a few knocks.

> In *Babes in the Wood* I was initiated into the mysteries of realism. The comedian wheeled me on to the stage in a pram. He tipped me up every night, and every night – I fell out. There was no make-believe in it. I did fall out. The people shouted with laughter, and the comedian was satisfied. It was his business to make them laugh. He did not pay any heed to the fact that, at every performance, I had black and blue marks all over me.

It was, of course, one way of dealing with pretty child actresses who might hog the comedy.

Gertie's practical working-class frugality (and the frugality of the theatre managers of the day) is underlined by the fact that she was wearing her own clothes.

> I remember I used to wear a blue dress in the 'lost in the wood' scene and as I had to sit on the stage I was always very careful to lift up my dress and sit on my little petticoat. The stage manager was very angry, and he used to scold me every time I did it. I thought it better to stand his scolding than to destroy my dress. You see my mother had *paid* for that dress, and I knew I had to be very careful of it.
>
> On that engagement I never got any salary – still I did not have any great hardship, for all the children playing in the pantomime lived with a matron who looked after us, and our meals, such as they were, were provided for us, so that we were not hungry.

From 1892 to 1900 she appeared in pantomime mostly in the provinces, but occasionally on the approaches to the London theatre – she played Dandini at the Fulham Grand in December of 1899. But in 1901 she was seen – and discovered – by Lionel Monckton.

There are some partnerships which once they have evolved seem inevitable. The delicate talents of Monckton and Gertie Millar were like a cobweb hanging from a branch on a sunlit autumn morning, with the early dew making it glisten like a diamond necklace. His music was full of lightness, charm and variety, while her voice and personality exactly matched the delicacy of his melodies. Constance Collier described Gertie Millar's voice as tiny and breathless, with the words half-spoken, half-sung. It was not only the singer and the song that matched one another – both matched the spirit of the age.

161

When a programme of Monckton's songs was heard on the television, the whole idea of pre-war 1914 songs was derided as being sentimental and ridiculous. It is difficult for a later generation, used to thirty years of peace, who have not seen their contemporaries disappear like the snows of yesteryear, to understand the catch in the heart which the very sound of these songs could bring. In 1952 Earl Winterton expressed the feeling which Gertie's songs gave to the survivors of the 1914 war. 'Personally I can never hear some of her most famous songs such as "They always call me Mary, but my name's Miss Gibbs" or "They never do that in Yorkshire", without deep emotion – for I think of the numerous friends with whom I went to hear them sung, and whose bones lie on the Somme, or in Gallipoli, or at the bottom of the Atlantic.'

Lionel Monckton saw Gertie Millar, and immediately knew that here was the girl who would bring his songs to life without destroying their essential quality.

'Lal' Monckton was forty when he saw and fell in love with Gertie Millar who was twenty-one. It was said that only a piano, and Gertie Millar could make him unbend. He had a curiously

Miss Gertie Millar in *The Orchid*: grace and sweetness

162

Lionel Monckton. A man of natural reserve

deliberate way of talking and a natural reserve, which was unusual in the days of open hearted 'jolly good chaps' and 'laddie boys' on the West End stage. That the endless variety of tunes which he produced which epitomised the gaiety of an extrovert generation should have come from a man so withdrawn was a curious contradiction. Sometimes, after a late supper at the Green Room Club, he would walk round to his house in Russell Square, go in, and wake up his dogs. He would then go out again, and walk the dogs round the darkened streets for hours, and if the moon were bright and the night fine, he would only get back at daylight.

Gertie Millar's first success was in *The Toreador*. George Grossmith Junior played the 'silly ass' part of Sir Archibald Slackit, a guards officer singing 'Everybody's awfully good to me'. The scenes – Susan's Flower Shop at Biarritz, and the Market Square at Villaya, Spain give a good idea of the settings, which were charming, as the girls were charming, and the tunes were charming.

But years afterwards when the piece was forgotten, the only thing which the audience remembered was the small part of the bridesmaid played by Gertie Millar and the song she sang, written by Monckton:

> At a wedding that is smart,
> If you want to lose your heart,
> Keep your eye on Cora, do.
> She's among the girls who glide
> In attendance on the bride.
> Keep your eye on Cora do!
> Such a modest little thing;
> But as soon as she approaches
> All the choir forget to sing,
> And the Parson when he ought to
> Keep his eye upon the ring,
> Well, he keeps his eye on Cora, too!
>
> Cora, Cora, Captivating Cora,
> Just a little bridesmaid for you all
> With a smile – ah
> Walking down the aisle – ah
> Captivating Cora
> Makes the Bride look small.'

In the same show she sang:

> Hi, little boys, hi little boys,
> Take care now,
> Keep off the grass,
> Keep off the grass,
> Quickly your hearts you must harden
> If she should sigh
> Don't catch her eye –
> Keep off the grass in the Garden.

The words and the songs suited the mood, and they suited the girl. It was said of her that not the least of her appeal was her complete lack of sauciness. She did not by intonation or gesture attempt to convey any suggestion of double meaning, her every movement being instinctive with grace and sweetness. Yet all this was backed up with a technique which had been learned in the hard school of provincial touring when she was a child.

In the same way Monckton himself was painstaking and careful. None of the success they achieved together was haphazard. Ellaline Terriss described Monckton's attitude towards his seemingly easy, rippling music. 'He took his time, altered, corrected and polished before he considered it was right. I have known him set a lyric over half a dozen times before he was satisfied. And he never admitted he *was* satisfied. But when he, with seeming reluctance, passed the number for rehearsal you could be sure you had something which the audience would applaud to the echo, hum all the way home – and remember for years and years to come . . . I was grateful to him for the songs he wrote for me. He would bring them to me, sit at the piano, and then carefully take off the magnificent diamond ring which he wore, placing it carefully on the lid. Then he would play the songs over . . . he had an innate air of distinction, and that got into his music.'

It was odd that a reserved, distinguished composer and the girl from Bradford should have made such a strong partnership, and a happy marriage.

From the moment she had been a bridesmaid, Gertie became the bride of the whole West End. She was the darling of the stalls and the gallery. In a very short time she had the rewards of her position. When she left the stage door after the last curtain call had been taken, the crowd fell back. They made a pathway for her. The men would take off their hats, and the women would look at her in wonder – perhaps slightly in envy. Suddenly the girl from Bradford

'A wonderful picture of the wedding dance' in *The Orchid*

was wrapped in sables or ermine, with the diamonds she wore glittering in the light of the street lamps. Smilingly she made her way to her brougham, or in later years to her car, with a quiet wave she was gone.

It was a time when queens of musical comedy were expected to behave royally, and to the end of her life Gertie always retained that slightly regal air which she had assumed when she had won her first success. The actresses of her day did not expect to have their clothes demolished by screaming fans. They had given pleasure, and in return they expected the respect due to their talent.

When Ruby Miller spoke on the radio about her time as a Gaiety girl the thing which she recalled with pleasure was the elegance of the past. No one was allowed in the stalls or boxes unless they were in evening dress. For the men that meant white tie, tails, satin-lined opera cape, a folding opera hat – and with white camellias in their buttonholes, carrying a silver knobbed ebony walking-stick, what a picture to remember with pleasure. The girls were as elegant as the men, with their complicated long trailing dresses, every tuck and stitch done by hand. 'If a dressmaker dared to copy your dress for someone else, you could sue them.'

George Edwardes, Ruby Miller remembered with equal pleasure, used to pay for the girls' dresses for the four days of Ascot. His Gaiety girls were to be leaders of fashion, not followers of other people's modes. 'On Ascot Sunday, the young men, dressed exquisitely in well-pressed white flannels with straw boaters poled us up and down the river. We lay on colourful cushions, protecting our complexions with huge sunshades of cerise or mauve. We were not supposed to get in the least bit sunburned, as a pink and white complexion was the thing which was admired. When we arrived at Boulters Lock, a crowd would be waiting for us, and they would sing the songs from our shows.'

It was against that background that Gertie Millar made her first successes. She was aware of her position, and expected others to respect it. When a minor manager kept her waiting in the corridor outside his office, she did not complain, she waited. But when she was shown into the office at last, she reduced the man to a jelly. How did he expect anyone to value her, his leading lady if *he* treated her like a servant? He made excuses, he blamed his staff. That was another thing, remarked Miss Millar shrewdly, if the staff behaved badly it was because they had been set a bad example! When the manager was a gibbering wreck, Miss Millar began to laugh. It was the last time she was treated with contempt.

From her first success in *The Toreador*, Gertie Millar never looked back – the names of the pieces in which she played, and the songs she sang, read like a pre-1914 history of the musical comedy stage. One of her greatest successes was in *Our Miss Gibbs*, when she played a mill-girl who became an assistant at a West End store, a favourite subject when so many polite and grand emporia were opening for the pleasure of the expanding middle classes and their families. The plot seems to have been a farrago of topicality and exaggeration – the Ascot Gold Cup was stolen, echoing a current news story, and the hero won the marathon at the newly resurrected Olympic Games. But the only memory which still lingered in the minds of those who saw the play was Gertie Millar singing: 'Moonstruck', written for her by her husband.

Ernest Short, like Noël Coward, described Gertie as a shimmering vision. 'At the White City in the last act Miss Millar was fantasy incarnate, wearing a dark blue satin pierrot costume with white pom-poms and a huge satin bow under the chin . . . then a bewitched little voice made its caressing chant felt through the half-light and a lithe form moved about the stage like a capful of invigorating wind off a summer sea.

> I'm such a silly when the moon comes out
> I hardly seem to know what I'm about,
> Skipping, hopping
> Never, never stopping.
>
> I'm all a-quiver when the moonbeams glance
> That is the moment when I long to dance
> I can never close a sleepy eye
> When the moon comes creeping up the sky.

Alas, the pincer claws of the war and the advance of jazz squeezed the old-fashioned charm of Gaiety musical comedy out of the West End. George Edwardes, caught by the war in Germany, was interned.

The last time Gertie Millar appeared on the stage was in 1918. She was not yet forty. Asked why she retired so soon she made a characteristic down-to-earth assessment of her popularity.

'In that last show in which I appeared, at a matinée, I noticed a sailor and his girl sitting in the front stalls. It was not usual then, but the best of luck to him – he was having his fling, and giving his girl the best he could. Nor did I mind at all when they cuddled one another. I did my little song, and my little dance. I got my applause and I came back to do my little dance again – and then I took my call. I looked at that sailor and his girl. They were looking at their programme to see who I was! Gertie, I said to myself, that's your cue. When they have to do that, it's time to make your exit. So I did.'

And she laughed.

It is not everyone who knows that their day is done and retires gracefully at the age of thirty-nine.

Gertie Millar always insisted that her success was due to the songs which her husband wrote for her. It is an unusual trait in people who have achieved great success to give the credit to others, but Gertie, like Gracie, was a generous, outgoing woman. She gave credit where it was due, and perhaps she knew that it did not take away from her talents to ascribe the setting in which they flourished as being the origin of the brilliance of the diamond.

Lionel Monckton died in 1924 when the sweetness and simplicity of his music was no longer appreciated.

After Monckton's death Gertie made a second happy marriage to the 2nd Earl of Dudley, a man who had had a distinguished career in politics as Lord Lieutenant of Ireland, and Governor General of Australia. She was not one to linger in the wings of the dusty theatre of the past once the curtain had come down. She made a new life for herself as a hostess, and filled her new role with distinction as she had filled her place on the stage with delicacy and verve.

Apart from the little piece on her first appearance, she wrote no autobiography. She was not interested in writing books or articles about her place in the theatre.

Occasionally all the old Gaiety girls who had married into the peerage foregathered for tea at the Ritz to talk over the past when the stage marrying into the peerage was an event. The 'girls' were all old and rich now, and they could look back over the past with no hint of bitterness. They had retired at the right time, before the future had eclipsed their past.

The last glimpse of Gertie Millar was at a Foyle's literary luncheon which was given to launch W. Macqueen Pope's book on the Gaiety Theatre. All the old stars from the past were there, including Miss Ellaline Terriss, who was determined to meet Gertie Millar whom she had never met before. Miss Terriss was also a lady dedicated to sentimental gestures, and she had brought 'Popie', as she called him, a present. It was a brick from the old Gaiety Theatre mounted in silver, which had belonged to her husband Seymour Hicks.

'I saw Gertie Millar,' wrote Ellaline Terriss, 'sitting on a settee looking round with that direct gaze of hers. I went up and introduced myself ... I showed her my bag, which contained the Gaiety brick. "I wonder if you can guess what I have in here?" I asked her. Gertie Millar looked at the bag. "I guess a bottle of gin." ' '

May 1924: Miss Gertie Millar, the former Gaiety actress, leaving the British Consulate in Paris with Lord Dudley after their marriage

Sentimentality about the past was not the forte of the girl from Bradford, yet somehow in her youth she had epitomised the sentiment of an age.

At the end of the Foyle's luncheon, which took place in the early 1950s, the old Gaiety ladies were cheered to the echo, and the people who had cheered them had tears in their eyes. Why?

Perhaps Noël Coward underlined the reason. 'Today everything Gertie Millar represented and signified has vanished along with so many gracious pleasures. Her quiet charm will live always in the hearts of those who saw her, and even when they too have gone away I think her legend will remain in the theatre where she meant so much, and was so much loved. When she retired from the stage a light went out. I shall always remember her lovingly and with gratitude.'

She remained, it was said, an enthusiast for the theatre to the end of her charmed and charming life.

Gertie Millar died in 1952, and even the list of her bequests – sable coat, diamond tiara, emerald and diamond necklace, Order of St. Patrick in diamonds, emeralds and rubies – echoes the age in which she lived – an opulent age in which the daughter of a mill-hand could become a countess, and be treated like a queen, for the sake of her smile, her dancing, and her breathless little voice.

The Gaiety girls have faded into a remote past. The estates and grandeur which were the stuff of their dreams seem like an old photograph album which records the sunlight of a forgotten age. Castle Ashby's broad acres and rich contents are threatened; Clumber House with its lake and its full rigged frigate, to which May Yohé once aspired, has crumbled to dust and disappeared; Hinton House, home of the Pouletts of Hinton St. George, once menaced by the organ grinder, has been turned into flats.

Romano's, Gatti's, the clubs where the crutch-and-toothpick boys gossiped about the lovely Belle and tried to ruin her life, the house in Avenue Road where the chivalrous Wertheimer used to drive Belle back from the Empire, even the Gaiety Theatre itself – all have disappeared into brick dust and rubble.

Sometimes when an orchestra plays one of the old tunes, or from an old programme the girls smile from under their flowery hats, the perfume of an age which delighted in charm comes alive for a short moment.

> Far away in Arcady
> Summer never passes
> Warm the wind that wanders free
> Through the bending grasses...
> There the birds have ever sung
> Arcady is always young....
>   Arcady, Arcady...

Monckton's melody is a lament for a vanished age.

SELECT BIBLIOGRAPHY

Agate, James, *Ego*, Hamish Hamilton, 1935
—— *Ego 2*, Gollancz, 1936
—— *Ego 3–9*, Harrap, 1938-48
—— *Those Were the Nights*, Hutchinson, 1946
Bishop, George, *My Betters*, Heinemann, 1957
Bolitho, Hector, *Marie Tempest*, Cobden-Sanderson, 1936
Booth, J. B., *London Town*, T. Werner Laurie, 1929
—— *Old Pink'Un Days*, Grant Richards, 1924
—— *Sporting Times, The Pink 'Un World etc.*, T. Werner Laurie, 1938
Coffin, Hayden, *Hayden Coffin's Book*, Alston Rivers, 1930
Egerton, William, *Faithful Memoirs of the Life, Amours and Performances of the justly Celebrated and most Eminent Actress of her Time, Mrs. Anne Oldfield*, London, 1731
Ervine, St. John, *The Theatre in my Time*, Rich & Cowan, 1933
Glasstone, Victor, *Victorian and Edwardian Theatres*, Thames & Hudson, 1975
Glover, Jimmy, *His Book*, Methuen, 1911
Grossmith, George, *G.G.*, Hutchinson, 1933
Hibbert, H. G., *Fifty Years of a Londoner's Life*, Grant Richards, 1916
Hicks, Seymour, *Between Ourselves*, Cassell, 1930
—— *Twenty-four Years of an Actor's Life*, Alston Rivers, 1910
—— *Vintage Years*, Cassell, 1943
Hollingshead, John, *Gaiety Chronicles*, Constable, 1898
—— *Good Old Gaiety*, London, 1903
Housman, Laurence, *The Duke of Flamborough*, Cape, 1928
Hyman, Alan, *The Gaiety Years*, Cassell, 1975
Kendall, Henry, *I Remember Romano's*, Macdonald, 1960
Mander, Raymond, and Mitchenson, Joe, *Lost Theatres of London*, Rupert Hart-Davis, 1968
—— *Victorian and Edwardian Entertainment*, Batsford, 1978
Maxim, Sir Hiram, *My Life*, Methuen, 1915
Nichols, Beverly, *Are they the same at Home?*, Cape, 1927
Pope, W. J. Macqueen, *Carriages at Eleven*, Hutchinson, 1947
—— *Gaiety Theatre of Enchantment*, W. H. Allen, 1949
—— *Ghosts and Greasepaint*, Robert Hale, 1951
—— *Nights of Gladness*, Hutchinson, 1956
—— *Shirt Fronts and Sables*, Hale, 1953
Public and Private Life of Mrs. Jordan by a Confidential Friend of the Departed, J. Duncombe, n.d.
Rosslyn, The Earl of, *My Gamble with Life*, Cassell, 1928
—— *Twice Captured*, Blackwood & Sons, 1900

Trewin, J. C., *Edwardian Theatre*, Blackwell, 1976
Saxe-Wyndham, Henry, *Annals of Covent Garden*, Chatto & Windus, 1906
Scott, Constance M., *Old Days in Bohemian London*, Hutchinson, 1919
Sheppard, Edgar, *George, Duke of Cambridge*, Longmans Green, 1907
Short, Ernest, *Fifty Years of Vaudeville*, Eyre & Spottiswoode, 1946
—— *Sixty Years of Theatre*, Eyre & Spottiswoode, 1951
Terriss, Ellaline, *Just a Little Bit of String*, Hutchinson, 1955
Vanbrugh, Irene, *To Tell my Story*, Hutchinson, 1948
Winn, Colin, C., *The Pouletts of Hinton St. George*, Research Publishing Company, 1976

Periodicals, Newspapers and other Sources
The court cases have been taken directly from the reports in *The Times* of the relevant dates.
The Bat, 31 March 1885 to 28 February 1888 (edited by James Davis)
The Gram, a South African P.O.W. Camp Magazine edited by the Earl of Rosslyn, several roneod copies in the Victoria and Albert Museum Library.
The Marie Tempest Jubilee Programme
Play Pictorials

INDEX

Abrahams (solicitor), 21
Acqui, Italy, 119
Actresses: and luxury, 7–8, 166; peerage, enlivening, 7; respectability, 1, 2, 3–9; status, 1–2, 166
Adelaide, Queen, 45, 46
Adelphi Theatre, 158
Adolphus, Prince, Duke of Cambridge, 44–5
Agate, James, 73–4, 76
Ainger, Arthur, 142
Albert, Prince Consort, 51, 54, 58
Alexandra, Queen, 30
Alhambra Theatre, 11
Archer, William, 82
Arnaud, Yvonne, 74
Augusta, Duchess of Cambridge, 44–5

Barnard, Charles, 11
Barnard, Mrs. Charles, 11
Barnard (solicitor), 91, 92
Bat, The, 129–38
Bateman, Mrs., 11
Bayley, Vera, 156–7
Beaufort, Henry Charles Fitzroy, 8th Duke, 132–8, 143
Beggar's Opera, 3
Belle of Cairo, The, 88–9
Bentinck, Lady Henry, 151
'Big Eight' (Gaiety girls), 4, 5–6
Bilton, Belle, 10–30, 171; marriage, 17–18, 19; divorce, 23, 24, 25–9; later life, 30
Bilton, Florence (Flo), 10–12, 13, 16, 17, 25
Bingham, William, *see* Compton
Bishop, George, 73
Blanche, John, 92

Blanche, Louisa, 92
Bluebell in Fairyland, 108
Boer War, 151–3
Bolitho, Hector, 60, 63, 69, 71, 73
Boucicault, Dion, 147–8
Bourchier, Arthur, 149, 153
Brooke, Daisy, Countess of, 141, 142
Bucknill, Judge, 121, 123
Buller, General, 151
Burlesque, 2–3, 127, 128
Byron, H. J., 3, 128

Café Royal, 15, 26
'Call Boy', 79, 80–1, 82
Cambridge, Duke of, *see* George, Prince, Duke of Cambridge
Carson, Sir Edward, 119, 122, 123
Caryll, Ivan, 82, 84
Caste, 147
Castle Ashby, Northants, 113, 115, 116, 120, 171
Charlotte, Princess of Wales, 44
Clancarty, Lord, 15, 16, 17; tries to annul son's marriage, 10, 18–19, 22, 23, 24, 28–9, 30
Clarke brothers, detectives, 21, 22, 23, 25, 26
Cleveland, Dowager Duchess, 99, 100, 103, 104
Clinton-Hope, Lord Francis Pelham-, *see* Pelham-Clinton-Hope, Lord Francis
Cloches de Corneville, Les, 11
'Clocks, The', 11
Clumber House, 84–6, 171
Collier, Constance, 161
Columbine, *see* Fairbrother, Louisa
Comedy Theatre, 67
Committee of Privileges, 107

174

176

in pantomime, 159–61; with Monckton, 161–8; retirement, 167–8
Miller, Rubby, 166
Mrs. Dot, 70
Mollison, William, 78
Monckton, Lionel, 161–8, 171
Moss, Daisy, *see* Markham
Munro, Kate, 66–7
Murphy (Q.C.), 37–8
Musical comedy, 3–5
Mystery of the Yellow Room, The, 124

Neilson, Julia, 63, 64, 70
Nevill, Lady Dorothy, 7
Newcastle, Duke of, 80, 84, 90, 91
Newman, Elizabeth, 95, 96, 98, 99–100, 107
Newspaper comment on divorce cases, 29–30, 42
Nicholson, William, 74
Nunn, Charles, 26–7

Oldfield, Anne, 2
On and Off, 79
Orkney, Edmond Walter Fitz-Maurice, 7th Earl, 126, 138–9
Osborne, Lord Alfred, 17, 19, 27–28
Our Miss Gibbs, 167

Pall Mall Gazette, 17, 18
Pantomime, 48
Peel, Capt., 54
Peile, Kinsey, 88
Pelham-Clinton-Hope, Lord Francis, 80, 84, 88–94
Pelican Club, 11
Penelope, 70
Pinero, Sir Arthur, 7, 91, 148
'Pipistrel', 130–2
Planché, J. R., 3
Play Pictorials, 4
Pope, W. Macqueen, *see* Macqueen Pope, W.
Poulett, Lady Bridget, 111
Poulett, Elizabeth Lavinia (Newman), *see* Newman, Elizabeth
Poulett, George Amias Fitzwarrine, 111
Poulett, Rosa, Countess, 100, 107

Poulett, William Henry, 6th Earl Poulett, 95–101, 102, 104–5
Poulett, William John Lydston, Viscount Hinton, 7th Earl Poulett, 95, 100, 104, 107, 108, 109, 110–11
Pounds, Louie, 4–5

Quaker Girl, The, 158
Queen's Necklace, The, 153

Raleigh, Cecil, 84, 88
Rawlings, Margaret, 74
Ray, Gabrielle, 4
Robertson, Tom, 147
Robinson, Anna, 153–5
Robinson, Mr., 16, 18
Romano's, 114, 115, 171
Ronald, Sir Landon, 74
Rosslyn, James Francis Harry St. Clair-Erskine, 5th Earl, 140–57; childhood, 141–2; Army, 142–3, 151–3; marriage, 143, 154–5, 157; gambling, 144–5, 146; bankruptcy, 146–7; stage career, 147–51, 153; journalism, 150–3
Royal Academy of Music, 62, 63, 64, 65
Royal Court Theatre, 88, 89
Russell, Sir C., 25–6, 37, 38, 41

St. Clair-Erskine, *see* Rosslyn
St. James's Theatre, London, 124
St. James's Theatre, Manchester, 160
Savoy Hotel, 8, 73
Scottish Life, 150
Searle, Mr., 25
Seven Castles, 50
Sheringham, George, 74
Shippy, Lydia Ann, *see* Turnour
Short, Ernest, 167
Shylock: or the Merchant of Venice Preserv'd, 2
Sims, George R., 84
Sisters Bilton, 11–12
Sketch, The, 82, 83, 89, 148, 159
Smith, Dodie, 76
Smith, F. E., 119
Smith, George Manby, 34–42
Smith, George Maslin, 35, 40
Smith, Mary Ann, 35, 40
Smith, Mary Anne, 39, 40–1, 42
Smith, Sarah Jane, 35, 40